The Palgrave Lacan Series

Series Editors
Calum Neill
Edinburgh Napier University
Scotland, UK

Derek Hook
Duquesne University
Pittsburgh, USA

Jacques Lacan is one of the most important and influential thinkers of the 20th century. The reach of this influence continues to grow as we settle into the 21st century, the resonance of Lacan's thought arguably only beginning now to be properly felt, both in terms of its application to clinical matters and in its application to a range of human activities and interests. The Palgrave Lacan Series is a book series for the best new writing in the Lacanian field, giving voice to the leading writers of a new generation of Lacanian thought. The series will comprise original monographs and thematic, multi-authored collections. The books in the series will explore aspects of Lacan's theory from new perspectives and with original insights. There will be books focused on particular areas of or issues in clinical work. There will be books focused on applying Lacanian theory to areas and issues beyond the clinic, to matters of society, politics, the arts and culture. Each book, whatever its particular concern, will work to expand our understanding of Lacan's theory and its value in the 21st century.

More information about this series at
http://www.palgrave.com/gp/series/15116

Duane Rousselle

Jacques Lacan and American Sociology

Be Wary of the Image

palgrave
macmillan

Duane Rousselle
Grand Valley State University
Allendale, MI, USA

The Palgrave Lacan Series
ISBN 978-3-030-19725-4 ISBN 978-3-030-19726-1 (eBook)
https://doi.org/10.1007/978-3-030-19726-1

Cover illustration: MirageC/Moment/Getty Images

This Palgrave Pivot imprint is published by the registered company Springer Nature Switzerland AG
The registered company address is: Gewerbestrasse 11, 6330 Cham, Switzerland

Contents

1	**Be Wary**	1
	References	8
2	**On Names**	11
	Freud's Proper Name	11
	From Proper Name to Name as Prop	16
	References	21
3	**Perverse America**	23
	American Wisdom	23
	Perverse Discourse and Capitalism	30
	References	38
4	**Early American Sociology**	41
	George Herbert Mead	41
	Charles Horton Cooley and Erving Goffman	52
	References	58
5	**On Strangers**	61
	Two Strangers	61
	Georg Simmel	64
	Ibn Khaldun	70
	References	74

6 Ways Forward 77
Alain Badiou's Choice 77
Parsing Talcott Parsons 83
References 90

Index 93

List of Figures

Fig. 3.1 Jacques Lacan's discourse of the university 31
Fig. 3.2 Jacques Lacan's capitalist discourse 32

List of Tables

Table 2.1	Clinical structures with their associated logical operations	19
Table 6.1	Talcott Parsons' systems	86
Table 6.2	Talcott Parsons' system levels	88

CHAPTER 1

Be Wary

Abstract This volume makes an intervention into American sociological discourse from within the Lacanian psychoanalytic orientation. This introduction explores the precise structure of discourse of American sociological theory and its pragmatist influences. It explores the possibility that the presentation of American sociological theory is structured in one of the two ways: as "university discourse" or as "capitalist discourse."

Keywords Sociological theory · American sociology · Capitalist discourse · Pragmatic sociology · Discourse theory

You can do interesting things with Lacanian psychoanalytic theory. Admittedly, this is a strange opening sentence for a Lacanian book about early American sociology. Truthfully, this book is not intended to teach the reader about the academic discipline of sociology. It is not meant to provide a coherent introduction or overview of the troubled relationship between psychoanalysis and sociology. Moreover, it is not meant to gather together some coherent and consistent body of knowledge about sociology (or even about Lacanian psychoanalytic theory). Rather, I would like to provide the reader with my objective up front: the aim of this book is to make an intervention into American sociological discourse from within the Lacanian psychoanalytic orientation. Thus, my orientation is psychoanalytic, and sociology shall merely serve as the field or environment within which

D. Rousselle, *Jacques Lacan and American Sociology*,
The Palgrave Lacan Series,
https://doi.org/10.1007/978-3-030-19726-1_1

I shall attempt to navigate. Or, rather, it is through psychoanalysis that I shall attempt to forge a new path forward within sociological discourse.

But why, then, do I intend to avoid coherent introductions, sustained overviews, and/or consistent bodies of knowledge? When knowledge is the agent of a discourse—that is, when, from the place of knowledge, there is an interrogation of that which has not yet been interrogated or not yet known—we can be sure that we are within what Jacques Lacan named the "university discourse." This is the discursive orientation found most often within graduate studies departments at Canadian and American universities. Take, for example, the following statement from the University of New Brunswick "Graduate Student Handbook" within the Department of Sociology (where I did two degrees): "[t]he thesis must be an original contribution to knowledge" (UNB Department of Sociology 2018: 9). Here, it is the "not yet known," the "not yet included," which is to be put to the service of knowledge. Or, as we shall see, it is the "non-part" of knowledge which must become rendered consistent with prior knowledge. This is the injunction of the university.

Many sociologists will be disappointed by this book precisely because it aims to frustrate the demand for a consistent body of knowledge. The academic sociologist might therefore inquire into the lack of comprehensiveness or into the various exclusions or lack of detail concerning several major early American sociologists such as Jane Addams, Lester F. Ward, Herbert Spencer, and others. Or perhaps the academic sociologist might expose an inadequacy in the various summaries of the work of George Herbert Mead, Talcott Parsons, C. Wright Mills, Erving Goffman, Charles Horton Cooley, or even, why not, Jacques Lacan. Similarly, an academic reader might protest that this text does not extensively delineate or explicate the various early schools of sociological thought such as conflict theory, structural-functionalism, systems theory, symbolic interactionism, applied sociology, and so on. My claim is that these demands demonstrate something important about the discourse from which the American sociologist is inevitably trained to speak: once again, we are returned to a discourse which demands for itself a consistency of knowledge.

I would like to mark a distinction between "analytic discourse" and "university discourse." The former is aimed at making an intervention into another discourse by engaging with its foundational presuppositions, and the latter intends only to increase the scope of its own knowledge (which is fundamentally built around an unacknowledged and latent presupposition). Thus, as Jacques-Alain Miller once put it, "one only understands what one thinks one already knows" (Miller 1990). Ecclesiastes states: "of making many books, it is a weariness of the flesh." It is what one *knows*, what one's ego can consolidate, that serves to protect the subject, fleetingly and provisionally, from an encounter with the real of castration anxiety.

Analytic discourse—when it succeeds—addresses a speaker who has been split by the presuppositions of his or her discourse. Put another way, the speaker of a discourse is always split between a fundamental presupposition and its foundational impossibility. This constitutes the "decisional structure" of university discourse. I am borrowing, for my own purposes, the language of Francois Laruelle who has described the project of "non-philosophy" in the following way: its project is one of locating the precise foundational decision, which had to be made within any consistent system of knowledge (in this case, it is philosophy) for it to be capable of speaking its own language, and exposing it as a bit of a fraud. Without the decisional apparatus, then, there is no constitution of knowledge (Laruelle 1999). It is through an interrogation of that split between the transcendental system of knowledge, grounded by a foundational assumption, and its primordial impossibility that the analytic discourse functions to reveal the centrality of castration.

American sociological discourse has since its birth been tormented by anxieties that are waiting for the subject behind any of his or her imaginary substitutions for castration. The American sociologist has been fascinated, captivated—captured even—by images which have at the same time stabilized and destabilized (as if in an endless tug of war) the social link. Analytic discourse moves in another direction and from a different point of departure. It consists of an obfuscation of any imaginary identification on the part of the subject so as to expose the split that exists within and against the hold of the image. The insistence of the imaginary registers a demand for consistency—a consistency in understanding the "self," or, more often, it is a consistency in the formation and explication of a knowledge. Indeed, the demand for consistency in knowledge is perhaps the imaginary fixation par excellence, and this is why Lacan so forcefully related knowledge and image. As Lola Lopez has put it, "the imaginary does not refer only to the image; the nucleus of the imaginary is consistency" (Lopez 2010).

American sociology has also been plagued by the ideology of capitalist pragmatism. The reader will no doubt wonder why I string these two words together: "capitalist" and "pragmatism." For now I will only open up the topic by suggesting that the reason the Freudian discovery—the "unconscious," or, more broadly, "psychoanalysis"—has never been at home within the American context has something to do with this equation: at the level of discourse, "capitalism" is roughly equivalent to "pragmatism." The discourse-centred approach that I introduce in this book makes this absolutely apparent: capitalism and pragmatism have the same discursive structure. And so too does American sociological discourse. Thus, American sociology is for the most part implicated in the discourse of capitalism.

The first sentence of this book was meant to lure American sociologists: "you can *do interesting things* with Lacanian psychoanalytic theory." I expect this statement to be appealing to American sociologists because it seems to respond to the demands of pragmatism: "*what can you do with your theory?*" Put another way: "*what is the 'cash-value' of your theory?*" In this case, the question concerns the cash-value of Lacanian theory for sociological inquiry. This was the expression of the American pragmatist William James, whose work has influenced many of the early sociologists. In particular, his work influenced sociologists working out of the hotspot of Chicago within a tradition that later became known as "symbolic interactionism." William James used the "cash-value" metaphor to argue that truth is defined precisely by its consequence: "does it work?", "can it be put to work?", and "can it be implemented within the chain of truths which have already been accepted as functional?" Bruce Kuklick explained that for James "a belief was true [only] if it worked for all of us, and guided us expeditiously through our semi-hospitable world. [...] Beliefs were ways of acting with reference to a precarious environment, and to say they were true was to say they were efficacious in this environment" (1981: xiv). The cash-value of truth helps us navigate this chaotic environment. It helps us in this environment which is precisely the phallic environment of the pervert who does not know whether or not the phallus has been castrated (and therefore opts for *both* castration and non-castration, or, in other words, disavowal of castration).

This implies not only that there is something capitalist about American pragmatism (and, by implication, American sociology), but that capitalism is, clinically speaking, perverse. I shall aim to demonstrate that Lacan's discovery of a fifth discourse (the first four discourses were "Mastery," "University," "Hysteria," and "Analytic") namely the discourse of capitalism, helps to orient us within American discourse. When we ask the question of the cash-value of Lacanian theory we are really asking about its social utility, or, to put it differently, we are asking how it might be put to use within sociology, and towards what end. Moreover, we are asking how it might be added to the accumulation of truths which have already been discovered within sociology. If a theory is to be accepted within American sociology it must demonstrate that it is capable of sliding into the body of knowledge that already exists. It must be rendered consistent as well as modular.

Some commentators have gone to great lengths to demonstrate that James' "cash-value" metaphor has little to do with capitalist pretensions (see for example Cotkin 1985). It is perhaps only by way of a discourse-centred perspective that the metaphor can finally be revealed as similar in structure to capitalist logic. Lacanian discourse theory assists us in articulating the logical relations that exist within pragmatist discourse—indeed, within the demand for "cash-value"—as being similar in form to capitalist discourse, but also similar in form to university discourse. However, there is an additional twist or mutation in the university discourse which brings about its capitalist variation: the demand to expound upon the cash-value of a given theory is similar to the demand one might read from university discourse, except that the excluded "non-part" must not essentially be brought into the consistency of knowledge (thereby making what was hitherto unknown more intelligible or believable), it must be capable of sliding itself in place of another piece of knowledge, another object of knowledge, that is, another theory. This is what I mean when I claim that theory within the American university must be "modular." Theories within America function as little gadgets or apps that one can call upon quickly to fulfil a certain function. Theory is meant to be plugged into an environment rather than to expose the essential structure of that environment.

In either case, knowledge, or theory, assists in the maintenance of a social link. The hope is that there will be another moment of insight to help guide further intellectual pursuits. In fact, there *must* be another moment of insight; it is *imperative that there be* another theory. This is why there are endless possibilities within contemporary sociological theory: "prosumer capitalism," "actor network theory," "queer theory," "intersectionality" all function as independent chapters in the supermarket of sociological theory which may be drawn upon on whim to enlighten *this* or *that* aspect of our social realities. Similar effects are produced in discussions concerning the various sociological methodologies or within debates concerning the various sociological "schools" or paradigms. The sociologist adopts a model of qualitative or quantitative research that can be quickly and easily "plugged into" an environment or field so as to produce the consequent knowledge that might mend the rupture in the social link. It is almost out of question within undergraduate and graduate sociology courses for the topic of methodology as such, that is, a deep study of the various methodological presuppositions (ontological, epistemological, and meta-ethical) to occur. On the contrary, a chapter of a sociological theory or sociological methodology textbook shall be dedicated to ontology and epistemology, so that a selection may be quickly made and then put to the side, so that the sociologist can get on with the more practical work of plugging him or herself back into society.

Paradoxically, the American sociologist is not at all tied to a consistent and coherent body of knowledge. Despite what the American sociologist believes, (s)he is not even tied to pragmatism as a philosophical body of knowledge. Pragmatism, in effect, forbids in advance the subject's immersion into its consistency of knowledge. This explains why early pragmatic influences within sociology are so rarely discussed in any detail within American sociology departments or within American sociological textbooks. If the American sociologist is not tied to pragmatism as a consistent and coherent body of knowledge, then how does (s)he nonetheless inhere within that body of knowledge? It seems to me that he or she is tied rather to an ideology of pragmatism, which implies that there are unconscious motivations at play. And these unconscious motivations have an obscure structure.

The unconscious is the agency responsible for the construction and perpetuation of discourse and yet its decisional structure operates as if at a distance from conscious speech, at a distance from its intensional discourse. Ideology therefore structures speech at the level of its form (rather than at the level of its content) by presenting it with a unique and distinctive grammar. This implies that ideology itself is the mechanism through which we come to understand all of social reality. Slavoj Žižek wrote that "it is not just a question of seeing things (that is, [of seeing] social reality) as they 'really are,' of throwing away the distorting spectacles of ideology; the main point is to see how the reality itself cannot reproduce itself without this so-called ideological mystification" (Žižek 1989: 24). American pragmatism effectively introduces into sociological discourse the fact of there being something like a discourse about social reality. Thus, it is not, as William James believed, that truth is what helps to orient us within our social environments. It is rather that truth is what fundamentally disturbs and yet nonetheless makes possible—indeed it produces, as a consequence of that disturbance—the necessity of our social environments. James so much demanded that truth anchor him within the chaotic social environment that he could not have admitted that the chaos of the social environment is itself the truth of his discourse.

We must aim to disrupt the hold that pragmatist ideology has had over American sociology by demonstrating that the social bond has always been founded upon a fundamental and primordial bankruptcy: social reality, the *real* of the social relationship is never reducible to the specular image, the "generalized other," roles, masks, performances, gestures, significant symbols, symbolic exchange, and so on. Truth is not, therefore, in the image as a stabilizing factor for any discourse within the social environment. Most of early American sociology has suffered—indeed, most of American discourse as such has suffered; and the implications are still felt today—from an inadequate account of the "symbolic" within the mental and social lives of the subject. Lacan's early teaching emphasized the role of the symbolic for the formation of discourse as such, and, moreover, for the establishment of a social link or bond for the subject. The social link is founded upon a symbolic paternal function which, put psychoanalytically, involves an initial radical universal prohibition of enjoyment. This aspect of the social bond has never been developed theoretically within the American context. Instead it is the "image," a product of the imaginary order, which takes charge over any symbolic function. The result: all sorts of problems have surfaced for psychoanalytic and sociological discourse within the United States.

At the same time, most of American sociology has suffered from an inability to think about what Alain Badiou refers to as the "immanence of truths," that is, the absolute truth of the real (see my transcription of his lecture: Rousselle 2018). So focused have the American sociologists been on insisting that "Freudian" drives are rooted in biology and/or nature that they have not been able to conceive of the later Lacanian corrective of the Real as that which resists symbolization, as the site of a profound *jouissance* (excessive stimulation). This is the reality of the Freudian drives, stated most forcefully in Freud's *Beyond The Pleasure Principle*. The consequence was that the symbolic and real dimensions of discourse became occluded, repressed, or, rather, disavowed.

American sociologists are so desperate for a social link that they hold onto a semblance of truth as the remnant of the image, an imaginary truth which would fleetingly rescue them from the chaos of the real. The irony is therefore that sociological discourse has suffered from the same problem it should have been charged with addressing: the inadequacy of a social link, and an aversion to understanding its unconscious and symptomatic dimensions.

The American sociologist, pragmatist, and conflict theorist, C. Wright Mills famously attacked the prevailing sociological paradigm of "Grand Theory" in his widely celebrated book *The Sociological Imagination* (1959). Put simply, Grand Theory problematically introduced a level of theoretical abstraction that obscured any understanding of (and applicability for) the social environment. Mills, in the second chapter of that book, began his attack on the work of the Harvard sociologist Talcott Parsons, whose theory was so obscure that Mills wondered if it could even be comprehended. The attack has had long-lasting effects on American sociology as we know it today. I hope that I am capable in my own way of making a similar gesture in the work that follows: my intention is to intervene into pragmatic sociology by calling for a return to the critical tradition of abstract theory.

Lacan will *not* serve as an orientation for us in our social environment. That, precisely, is his promise.

References

Cotkin, George. 1985. William James and the Cash-Value Metaphor. *ETC: A Review of General Semantics* 42 (1): 37–46.

Kuklick, Bruce. 1981. Introduction. In *Pragmatism* (William James). Cambridge: Cambridge University Press.

Laruelle, Francios. 1999. A Summary of Non-Philosophy. *Pli: The Warwick Journal of Philosophy* 8: 138–148.

Lopez, Lola. 2010. The Body: Consistency of the *Speaking-Being*. As Retrieved on August 17, 2018 from https://www.champlacanien.net/public/docu/2/rdv2010pre3.pdf.

Miller, Jacques-Alain. 1990. Micro-scopia: An Introduction to the Reading of Television. In *Television: A Challenge to the Psychoanalytic Establishment*, trans. Denis Hollier, Rosalind Krauss, Annette Michelson, and Jeffrey Mehlmen and ed. Joan Copjec, xi–xxx. New York, NY: W. W. Norton.

Rousselle, Duane. 2018. Transcription on the Immanence of Truths. *DingPolitik*. As Retrieved on October 26, 2018 from https://dingpolitik.wordpress.com/2018/10/23/alain-badiou-lecture-on-the-immanence-of-truth-transcription/.

UNB Department of Sociology. 2018. Department of Sociology Graduate Student Handbook. As Retrieved on July 28, 2018 from https://www.unb.ca/fredericton/arts/_assets/documents/soc-gradhandbook.pdf.

Žižek, Slavoj. 1989. *The Sublime Object of Ideology*. New York, NY: Verso Books.

CHAPTER 2

On Names

Abstract American sociologists were involved in a project of patching together a sociology that worked for them. The consequence has been that sociologists lost hold of a truly valuable legacy that might have promoted the sort of quality of mind required for critical sociological engagement. We can learn a lot about sociology within American by observing the way that some of the American sociologists related to the Freudian discovery. This chapter explores the function of Freud's name during his lectures at Clark University. My claim is that American sociology—indeed America as such—both accepted *and* rejected the Freudian discovery.

Keywords Freud · American psychoanalysis · Perversion · American sociology · Lacanian psychoanalysis

Freud's Proper Name

Early American sociologists created their own distinctive flavour of sociological theory. However, their key reference points were imported in chunks from the French, British, and German contexts. For example, William Graham Sumner (1840–1910) integrated the work of Auguste Comte (France) and Herbert Spencer (United Kingdom) into one of his courses at Yale University (Connecticut, United States of America).

D. Rousselle, *Jacques Lacan and American Sociology*,
The Palgrave Lacan Series,
https://doi.org/10.1007/978-3-030-19726-1_2

A key course in sociology was also taught by Frank Wilson Blackmar at the University of Kansas in 1890, aptly titled "Elements of Sociology." It was in 1892 that the first department of sociology was established at the University of Chicago, and, in 1895 the American *Journal of Sociology* was inaugurated with the University of Chicago Press. Lester Ward, first president of the American Sociological Association (1906), cited key texts written by Auguste Comte and Herbert Spencer more than two hundred times each in the first volume of his influential *Dynamic Sociology* ([1893] 1911).

In every case, early American sociologists were involved in a project of patching together a sociology that worked for them. C. Wright Mills, in his widely influential book *The Sociological Imagination*, claimed that American sociology operated according to a curious process of "amalgamation." He wrote:

> The peculiarities of sociology may be understood as distortions of one or more of its traditional tendencies. But its promises may also be understood in terms of these tendencies. In the United States today there has come about a sort of Hellenistic amalgamation, embodying various elements and aims from the sociologies of the several Western societies. (Mills 1959: 24)

C. Wright Mills believed that these amalgamations were distorting sociological inquiry. Later, in 1975, a young George Ritzer arrived on the scene and argued that sociology must be understood as inherently "a multiple paradigm science" (Ritzer 1974). It is seldom acknowledged by scholars, and not at all explored by them, that Mills cautioned against this approach: "[t]he danger is that amidst such sociological abundance, other social scientists will become so impatient, and sociologists be in such a hurry for 'research,' that they will lose hold of a truly valuable legacy" (1959: 24). Sociology is for Mills a problem when it is "impatient," "in a hurry," in a position of "abundance." The consequence is that sociologists "lose hold of a truly valuable legacy" that might promise the sort of "quality of mind" required for pragmatic sociological engagement.

The sociologist is imagined here as a bit of an addict, sweating from the "quick fix" of the next big thing, constantly sliding through the various bodies of literature that seem pop up here and there, whose theoretical perspectives or paradigms rise and fall like so many fashionable commodities sold at the hip stores in the shopping malls. There is nonetheless a desperate attempt to defend the contours of the Western academic tradition of sociology against other possible trends in non-European sociology. Yet, the "non-European" sociological imagination precedes the European one by centuries: for example, there is the curious case of ibn Khaldun (Dhaouadi 1990).

The work of ibn Khaldun demonstrates not only that the sociological imagination was in full swing in the middle east during the 1300s, but that that sort of imagination goes beyond much of the work that we see in modern sociological theory. For example, ibn Khaldun's work demonstrates a profound awareness of the importance of language—and, moreover, of the transformative power of ambiguity, polyvalence, metaphor, and so on—as well as the essential conflict that exists between elements in a "social geometry" (to borrow a later expression from Georg Simmel). Between the sedentary population and the periphery there is an essential asymmetry, and an essential rift, which Jacques Lacan would have related to the impossible sexual relationship. Moreover, those at the centre of the social bond (*'asabiyyah*) eventually fall into moral decadence. The bond becomes more fragile, and group loyalty breaks down. Those on the periphery of the social bond are in the meantime forming a new social bond, a new morality, as they move their way back towards the centre. This cyclical understanding of the social bond is remarkable and offers itself as a nice corrective to the resource-based conflict theory of somebody like Karl Marx. Whereas traditional Marxist accounts of conflict focus on resource (a logic of "having" or "not having"), ibn Khaldun's perspective focuses on the difference of social location. Incidentally, is it not today, precisely, that the Marxist account is being transformed by Lacanian Marxists into a social topology/geometry? Those *without* resources are on the periphery of the social bond (Jacques Ranciere would name them the "non-part") and those *with* resources, *with* ownership of the means of production, are in the centre of the social bond (Alain Badiou would suggest that they constitute the fundamental operation of "the count," since they are responsible for legislating "the possible" within a given social-political situation). One wonders to what extent sociological theorists today might benefit from a return to the "social geometry" of conflict laid out not only by Georg Simmel and ibn Khaldun but also less obviously in the work of C. Wright Mills, Karl Marx, and others.

The American sociologist today opposes any serious disciplinary conviction while nonetheless defending the European roots: French (Montesquieu, Comte, Durkheim), German (Weber, Simmel, Marx), and British (Herbert Spencer). For example, the American school of "symbolic interactionism" is often used to frame all discussions in undergraduate and graduate student days in sociology. Indeed, symbolic interactionism has, in one way or another, become an exemplary American *style*—though by no means the *only* style—of sociology, akin, in some respects, to *applied sociology*. In any case, one wonders if the discipline of sociology can survive within America, or whether it will eventually burn itself out. My claim is that these are the only two options on the table. Paradoxically, the problems with American sociology have more to do with the discourse through which it speaks rather than with the discourses it aims to study (e.g., political, cultural, situational, etc.). I aim to demonstrate that the discourses it aims to study are in some sense indifferent to the discourse upon which they are studied.

I believe that we can learn a lot about sociological discourse within America by observing the way that some of the American sociologists related to the Freudian discovery. Sigmund Freud (1856–1939), the father of psychoanalysis, was invited into the United States by G. Stanley Hall in 1909 to present a series of introductory lectures on psychoanalysis at Clark University in Worcester, Massachusetts. Despite the warm reception, Freud observed a general aversion to psychoanalytic discourse from his audience. It was within the context of this general reticence to psychoanalysis that the emergent discipline of American sociology confronted the Freudian discovery. The American sociologists accepted psychoanalytic theory in piecemeal at best, thereby neglecting its deeper offerings and insights. There has yet to be written any serious exploration of this missed encounter from the perspective of psychoanalytic discourse theory. It seems to me that contemporary Lacanian discourse theory introduces the most innovative and important reading of this missed encounter. For this reason, I have set for myself the task of providing some provisional reference points from within the Lacanian orientation.

My position is that Freud's remarks at Clark University were of less importance than the function of his proper name. His intuition seldom strayed from pivotal psychoanalytic concerns. In this case, his opening statement was indicative: "I assume I owe this honour to the association of my name with the theme of psychoanalysis, and consequently it is of psychoanalysis that I shall aim to speak" (Freud [1912] 1910). This statement followed from another: "[i]t is a new and somewhat embarrassing experience for me to appear as a lecturer before students of the New World" (Freud [1912] 1910). It seems to me that Freud's proper name underwent considerable devaluation within the United States. Indeed, he seemed concerned with this devaluation: he was not only embarrassed to be speaking in front of this audience, he was also distressed because they insistently referred to him as "Sigmund" rather than "Dr. Freud" (see Hartley 2018; Freud [1912] 1910). Thus, more should be written about the logic and function of this degradation and its subsequent implications for psychoanalytic discourse within the American continent.

A psychoanalytic situation has never really existed within the United States (see Svolos 2017: 221, et passim; also, see Rousselle 2018). Although Freud noted that psychoanalysis became popular among the lay public and that it found its way into medical psychiatric training programmes, it nonetheless "suffered a great deal from being watered down" (Freud 1925: 15). Its potential intervention was blunted by the proliferation of theories and techniques "which [had] no relation to it [but found] cover under its name" (Freud 1925: 15). Svolos has even claimed that the "Americans did not accept psychoanalysis as psychoanalysis, but as Freudianism, a practice modelled after Freud's ego, or Freud's desire […]" (2017: 231). Svolos argued that American psychoanalysts were more fascinated by imaginary substitutes for psychoanalysis, that is, by the image of Freud (his ego and his *persona*), rather than his technique. Problematically, this paved the way for the development of a wide assortment of ineffectual therapies within a "Psy" market; such as, for example, cognitive behavioural therapy, mindfulness, play therapy, dialectical behavioural therapy, and so on. Psychoanalysis proper was rendered inadequate in the American context.

But what did psychoanalysis become? On the one hand, it is not clear that it was rejected entirely. On the other hand, it is not clear that psychoanalysis was accepted in its entirety—there was obvious resistance. There was a strange general acceptance of the rejection of psychoanalysis, and this aversion to psychoanalysis took place primarily within the orientation of the market. Thus, Jacques-Alain Miller, founding member of the School of the Freudian Cause as well as the World Association of Psychoanalysis, wrote: "I conclude: there is [now] a mental market" (Miller 2005: 7). Psychoanalysis became within America an object for exchange: it was incorporated into the mental market.

From Proper Name to Name as Prop

We should take an essential detour through Jacques Lacan's theory of proper names. For Lacan, the function of a proper name is to inaugurate a coherent and consistent body of knowledge. Lacan was acutely aware of Ferdinand de Saussure's semiological theory which proposed that speech is composed of minimal units of meaning, and that, a sign is what unites a signifier and signified (Saussure [1916] 1959). Saussure's structuralist semiology (or semiotics) became the basis for a whole new world of social and cultural theory, as exemplified, for example, in the work of the French mythologist Roland Barthes. Put simply, a signifier has as its function to provide an index or an anchor for meaning; the signifier does not have any meaning in and of itself.

Lacan advanced a bit further than the semiologists by claiming that a proper name occupies the position and function of master signifier (see Ragland 2015: 65; Soler 2016: 94–95). This may be formalized in the following way: S1 → S2. S1, in the preceding formula, indicates the proper name as master signifier, and the arrow indicates that the master signifier strives to address or otherwise produce for itself a body of meaning or a coherent network of signifiers (S2). In Lacan's twenty-third seminar, *Le Sinthome*, he remarked that "the proper noun does all it can to make itself more than the S1, the master's signifier, which heads toward the S that I've labelled with the index of a subscript 2, which is that around which the gist of knowledge accumulates: S1 → S2 ([1975–1976] 2016: 73).

It seems to me that a shift occurred somewhere between Lacan's third (1955) and twenty-third seminars (1975). This shift is best located in his theory of the proper name, or, rather, it can be found in his theory of the "name-of-the-father." During the period of the third seminar Lacan took the following position: "I will thus take *Verwerfung* to be 'foreclosure' of the signifier [...] at the point at which the name-of-the-father is summoned [...] a pure and simple hole may thus answer" ([1955] 2006: 466). Psychosis, which is a condition of absolutely rejecting the social link, of absolutely rejecting discourse, involves the foreclosure of the name-of-the-father as master signifier.

We can detect a discrete binary clinical classification whereby the subject's confinement is to either the one or the other mental or discursive structure: either neurosis, whereby a discourse is accepted, or else psychosis, the rejection of discourse (Miller 2009). The analytical task was only to discern whether the name-of-the-father was adequate or inadequate for the purposes of discourse as a social link. But a radically new possibility presented itself in Lacan's twenty-third seminar. The twenty-third seminar achieved the possibility of there being a non-binary clinic, a clinic which maintains that there may be some obscurity concerning the absence or presence of the name-of-the-father. In this case, the underlying clinical structure cannot easily be classified as ***either*** neurotic *or else* psychotic. Jacques-Alain Miller put it like this: "[there was] a Lacanian credo [...]: 'I baptize you neurotic if there is the Name-of-the-Father, I baptize you psychotic if the Name-of-the-Father isn't there'" (Miller 2009: 148).

The implications of the non-binary clinic are such that the analyst may now make use of a third classification, that of "ordinary psychosis" (Miller 2009). In cases of ordinary psychosis, the analyst locates "discrete signs" via the "threefold externalities" of "society, body, and subject" (ibid.: 155–158). "Social externality" refers to the subject's inability to identify with any social bond—it is an inability to maintain a social link with others; "bodily externality" implies a disconnection or disjuncture with the body—it is no longer "my" body (in the sense of "having" a body), and; "subjective externality" refers to the subject's radical emptiness within language (ibid.). In any case, the lesson for us is crucial: a subject can do without the proper name-of-the-father, provided that it is made use of as a master signifier (Lacan, n.d.: 84). Miller put it like this: "[s]o, the question is of the Name-of-the-Father as predicate. This means that it's a substituted substitute" (Miller 2009: 153). When this possibility occurs, that is, when the name-of-the-father may or may not have been foreclosed, or, rather, when, within the symbolic, there appears only a hole, the subject may turn towards any semblance of a father, any particular master signifier, to make use of it as a prop for the establishment of a discourse (Miller in Lacan 2003). This is why Lacan used the expression "pere-version," a French homophone of "perversion:" it was to indicate the subject's "turn toward the father" (Lacan [1974] 2018: 29). On the other hand, the neurotic is constantly trying to turn ***against*** the father. And, indeed, the psychotic is radically ***without*** a father.

We should be very precise: ordinary psychosis and perversion are fundamentally different clinical realities. The former operates according to a logic of foreclosure of the name-of-the-father, while the latter operates according to a logic of disavowal of castration. But we should nonetheless ask ourselves why, for Jacques-Alain Miller, perversion was removed as a serious clinical category at precisely the same moment that the discovery of a new clinical structure, that of ordinary psychosis, arrived on the scene. Note the following series of statements from Jacques-Alain Miller:

> I observed that we essentially had a binary clinic for years, which was neurosis or psychosis. An either/or, an absolute either/or. Well, you also had perversion, but it didn't weigh on the same scale, essentially because true perverts don't really analyze themselves, so what you have in analysis are subjects with perverse traits. Perversion is a questionable term which has been put into disarray by the gay movement, and so tends to be a discarded category. So our clinic had an essentially binary character. (Miller 2009: 147)

Perhaps the way forward for us is to continue to think the clinical question of perverse structure by focusing on the later Lacanian discovery of "capitalist discourse" (Lacan 1972). The traditional view—the earlier Lacanian view—was that there are four discourses: Master, University, Hysteric, and Analyst. The capitalist discourse appears later as a "mutation," a "fifth discourse." Some commentators read the "capitalist discourse" as an exemplary form of psychotic stabilization, that is, as an ordinary psychosis. For example, Stijn Vanheule has written the following: "[i]n my opinion, the capitalist discourse promotes a specific type of semblance that might function as a support in psychosis: the persona of the consumer who checks the market for solutions that might solve dissatisfaction" (Vanheule 2016). Here we can discern the possibility that capitalist discourse functions as a means of stabilization for psychotic subjects.

On the other hand, Slavoj Žižek has claimed that the American capitalist social bond expresses a fundamentally perverse structure. He wrote that "[f]rom the libidinal standpoint, capitalism is a regime of perversion, not psychosis: it disavows castration, it does not exclude or suspend it" (Žižek 2017). The capitalist is not, therefore, a psychotic who has found a mode of stabilization but is rather a pervert who oscillates between castration and denial of castration. Thus, there are two possibilities: capitalism as perversion or capitalism as psychosis.

I return for the moment to the American encounter with Freudian psychoanalysis. Lacan said that "[Freud imported into America] a discourse that would finally be truly pestilent, wholly devoted, finally, to the service of capitalist discourse" (Lacan 1972). Does this not imply that Freud's discourse was not at all prepared to make an intervention in America? If the first possibility was that American academics and practitioners foreclosed Freud's proper name, so that the structural consequence was the eclipse of psychoanalytic discourse within the United States—then the second possibility was that the Americans disavowed the Freudian unconscious.

It seems to me that this second possibility is much more likely. Indeed, the evidence suggests that the American simultaneously accepted *and* rejected the Freudian discovery. To be even more precise, they both accepted as well as rejected—which means *disavowed*—castration anxiety. This, precisely, is the logical operation we find associated with the perverse clinical structure. For neurosis, there is a logical negation articulated by "repression," for perversion, there is a logical negation articulated by "disavowal," and for psychosis, there is a logical negation articulated by "foreclosure" (Table 2.1).

Perversion is often neglected as a clinical structure by clinicians. We have seen evidence of this already from Jacques-Alain Miller. It has been neglected particularly within the binary clinic of neurosis *or* psychosis. The perverse subject constitutes for himself a discourse and social bond only by turning towards and making use of a master signifier as a prop. When the name-of-the-father is revealed as inadequate it is possible that the subject simultaneously accepts *and* rejects, which is to say that the subject disavows castration. Žižek's position has been that the United States is fundamentally a "regime of perversion" which operates according to a logic of disavowal (Žižek 2017: 482). The pervert's essential statement is: "I know very well [that I am castrated,] but I shall act as if I did not know this." This position, as the discursive dominant of the American social bond, seems better supported by the evidence.

The question I want now to pursue concerns the anchorage of knowledge or meaning within perverse discourse. Provisionally, we might claim

Table 2.1 Clinical structures with their associated logical operations

Clinical structure	*Operation*
Neurosis	Repression
Perversion	Disavowal
Psychosis	Foreclosure

that S2 becomes anchored to any number of master signifiers, where each S1 offers the subject an instrumental solution to the breakage or rupture in the social link (Vanheule 2016). I propose the following formula: $ → S1 → S2. This formula expresses subjective division, castration, as $, which is disavowed (it is simultaneously rejected and accepted as the agent of the discourse). The subject turns towards a master signifier, S1, as a prop for the production of, and gateway into, a consistency of knowledge and meaning, S2. Thus, within the American context we sense the importance of fraternities, sports teams, subcultural politics, group therapy, and so on, all of which are imaginary forms of identification which provisionally and fleetingly anchor the social bond. Indeed, these forms of identification offer subjects inventive imaginary solutions to the profound and traumatic feeling of destitution. However, destitution is nonetheless simultaneously anticipated, refuted, engaged, and re-engaged.

The missing S1 is rendered in real-time as an imaginary semblance. Wilson C. McWilliams, in his classic volume *The Idea of Fraternity in America* (1973), wrote that "Americans, especially young Americans, cannot find their country in the land about them [...]," and "[within the fraternities,] which Americans have made for themselves, we can learn to see our countrymen. We can recognize that our torments are common, [...] if one is fortunate, he may even find a brother among his fellow Americans" (McWilliams 1992: x). Freemasons, the "all-seeing eye," Hollywood, ... these are all concepts associated with the image, with the gaze, that is, with the object of the scopic drive, in America. The idea of fraternity within the university demonstrates something crucial about the discursive structure of the American people: do you trust what you see? Or, is there some sort of conspiracy obscuring the full image? As Slavoj Žižek has put it: "[we] are called to decide, while, at the same time, receiving the message that [we] are in no position to effectively decide [...] The recourse to 'conspiracy theories' is a desperate way out of this deadlock [...]" (Žižek 1999). Conspiracy theory is here understood as an expression of perversity.

At the heart of American discourse there is, finally, the following pragmatic position concerning knowledge: the truthfulness of a proposition is related fundamentally to its social utility, or, rather, to its social usefulness. This may be discovered in the work of Charles Sanders Peirce (the so-called "pragmatic maxim," which is already a paradoxical term illustrating a certain disavowal), John Dewey (the notion of practical "truth" as the core of philosophical pragmatism), and William James, among others. However, we might also observe this discursive structure within popular American culture: it is the aesthetic of American wisdom spread far and wide.

References

Dhaouadi, Mahmoud. 1990. Ibn Khaldun: The Founding Father of Eastern Sociology. *International Sociology* 5 (3): 319–335.

Freud, Sigmund. [1912] 1910. Five Lectures on Psychoanalysis. *American Journal of Psychology* 21. As Retrieved on May 9, 2018 from https://www.rasch.org/over.htm.

Freud, Sigmund. 1925. *An Autobiographical Study*. As Retrieved on May 23, 2018 from http://www.mhweb.org/mpc_course/freud.pdf.

Hartley, Dale. 2018. Sigmund Freud Hated America: 5 Reasons Why. *Psychology Today*, January 9. As Retrieved on May 15, 2018 from https://www.psychologytoday.com/us/blog/machiavellians-gulling-the-rubes/201801/sigmund-freud-hated-america-5-reasons-why.

Lacan, Jacques. n.d. *Le Sinthome*. As Retrieved on June 6, 2018 from http://staferla.free.fr/S23/S23%20LE%20SINTHOME.pdf.

Lacan, Jacques. 1972. *On Psychoanalytic Discourse*, trans. Jack. W. Stone. As Retrieved on June 14, 2018 from http://aaaaarg.fail/upload/jacques-lacan-on-psychoanalytic-discourse-1.pdf.

Lacan, Jacques. 2003. *On the Names-of-the-Father*, trans. Bruce Fink and Jacques-Alain Miller. New York, NY: Polity Books.

Lacan, Jacques. [1955] 2006. On a Question Prior to Any Possible Treatment of Psychosis. In *Ecrits*, trans. Bruce Fink and ed. Jacques-Alain Miller. New York: W. W. Norton.

Lacan, Jacques. [1975–1976] 2016. *The Seminar of Jacques Lacan, Book XXIII: The Sinthome*, trans. Adrian Price and ed. Jacques-Alain Miller. Malden, MA: Polity Press.

McWilliams, Wilson. 1992. *The Idea of Fraternity in America*. Berkeley: University of California Press.

Miller, Jacques-Alain. 2005. The Mental Market. *Lacanian Praxis: International Quarterly of Applied Psychoanalysis* 2 (November): 5–7.

Miller, Jacques-Alain. 2009. Ordinary Psychosis Revisited. *Psychoanalytic Notebooks* 19. As Retrieved on June 7, 2018 from https://www.wapa.com.au/uploads/3/2/1/1/32113275/jacques-alain_miller_ordinary_psychosis.pdf.

Mills, C. Wright. 1959. *The Sociological Imagination*. Oxford: Oxford University Press.

Ragland, Ellie. 2015. Some Reflections on Lacan's Theory of Discourse Structures as Set Out in 'To Jakobson'. In *Jacques Lacan and the Logic of Structure: Topology and Language in Psychoanalysis*, ed. Ellie Ragland, 45–77. New York: Routledge.

Ritzer, George. 1974. *Sociology: A Multiple Paradigm Science*. Boston: Allyn & Bacon.

Rousselle, Duane. 2018. Lacanian Psychoanalysis in the Twenty-First Century. *Psychoanalytic Discourse* 5. See http://www.psychoanalyticdiscourse.com.

de Saussure, Ferdinand. [1916] 1959. *Course in General Linguistics*, trans. Wade Baskin and ed. Charles Bally and Albert Sechehaye. New York, NY: The Philosophical Library.

Soler, Colette. 2016. *Lacanian Affects: The Function of Affect in Lacan's Work*. New York, NY: Routledge.

Svolos, Thomas. 2017. *Twenty-First Century Psychoanalysis*. London: Karnac Books.

Vanheule, Stijn. 2016. Capitalist Discourse, Subjectivity and Lacanian Psychoanalysis. *Frontiers in Psychology* 7. As Retrieved on June 7, 2018 from https://www.frontiersin.org/articles/10.3389/fpsyg.2016.01948/full.

Ward, Lester. [1883] 1911. *Dynamic Sociology*, Vol. 1. New York: D. Appleton & Company.

Žižek, Slavoj. 1999. You May! *London Review of Books* 21 (6): 3–6.

Žižek, Slavoj. 2017. Can One Exit the Capitalist's Discourse Without Becoming a Saint? *Crisis & Critique* 3 (1): 481–499.

CHAPTER 3

Perverse America

Abstract This chapter explores various examples of "American Wisdom." American wisdom is a fragmented structure of discourse which currently prevails within American society. On social media, printed on bubble gum wrappings, on the sleeves of coffee cups, and so on, there are symbolic inscriptions which are meant to retroactively alleviate the real trauma of subjective destitution. Lacanian clinicians have also noted that this is the discursive structure of addictions. Addiction is not only epidemic within America, but it is probably what is most American about America. Within America, the universal prohibition of the father has been replaced with the particular affirmative declarations of the maternal superegoic voice.

Keywords Postmodernism · American aesthetics · American culture · Lacanian psychoanalysis · Perversion · Psychosis · Capitalist discourse

American Wisdom

Consider the popular American television drama *Grey's Anatomy* (2005–2018). The medical drama (including all of its props, setting, narrative, roles, and so on) serves as a pretence to both conceal and reveal fundamental traumatic questions concerning sexuality and death. I have argued elsewhere that all discourses are reducible to key questions

D. Rousselle, *Jacques Lacan and American Sociology*,
The Palgrave Lacan Series,
https://doi.org/10.1007/978-3-030-19726-1_3

concerning sexuality and death, such as "what does it mean to be a woman?," "am I alive or am I dead?," or "can I master death?" (see Rousselle 2013). Indeed, difficult questions concerning either sexuality or death (or both) are most often discovered in cases of hysterical or obsessional neurosis. These unanswerable questions seem to pose the most enduring challenge to our mental well-being and therefore disrupt the consistency of our everyday life. These questions are "real" in the Lacanian sense: they shatter the symbolic coordinates of our everyday lives, they disrupt its imaginary consistency, introducing an essential impasse, an obstacle, a rupture.

These are the questions that are rendered most palpable and witnessed as entirely unavoidable within *Grey's Anatomy*. Each episode reaches a fever pitch at the precise moment that a fundamental question concerning sexuality or mortality becomes no longer containable within the medical pretence. This is most often indicated by an intensification in background music. Consequently, the medical pretence momentarily dissolves as the music comes to an abrupt and dramatic halt. It is at this crucial moment that the subject of the film traumatically, though fleetingly, encounters truth: the subject is revealed in his or her destitution, incapable of finding a solution to the problem. Suddenly, a calm reassuring female voice speaks from somewhere outside of the frame—as if from another scene—to provide us all with an essential life lesson.

We should pay close attention to these little life lessons because they reveal to us something essential about life in America. Each lesson functions as a little piece of wisdom meant to retroactively offer a remedy, however provisional, for subjective destitution. We are treated to such life lessons as: "sometimes the expected simply pales in comparison to the unexpected," "sometimes it is good to be scared, it means you still have something to lose," "sometimes the future changes quickly and completely and we're left with only the choice of what to do next," and so on. These life lessons introduce the triumph of the imaginary against the trauma of the real. Within the shit-storm of the plot, there is, finally, some calm, quiet, reassurance.

Grey's Anatomy demonstrates how capitalist discourse functions today, and, moreover how Meredith Grey, a female doctor, can come to embody the most essential anatomy, the maternal phallus: the paternal signifier, that is, the "name-of-the-father," would have instigated a universal prohibition against enjoyment (e.g., "you shall not …"), and this would have, as a consequence, instigated a desire to return to the supposed lost enjoyment. That was the classical Freudian model. The master discourse of capitalism—Lacan claimed that it was the "new" master discourse during his 1972 seminars—substitutes the universal paternal symbolic prohibition for a maternal cinematic superegoic voice. The latter speaks to the subject through the a particular affirmative logic. It is a shift from the ***universal prohibition of enjoyment*** to a ***particular affirmative injunction to enjoy***. Moreover, it is a shift from the statement "you shall not …" to "sometimes you should …" (or "maybe it is okay that …"). Slavoj Žižek (1999) argues that it is a shift from the symbolic prohibition of enjoyment towards an imaginary imperative to enjoy.

Slavoj Žižek asks: "does the capitalist injunction to enjoy effectively aim at soliciting *jouissance* in its excessive character, or are we ultimately rather dealing with a kind of universalized pleasure-principle, with a life dedicated to pleasures?" He continues, "[i]n other words, are the injunctions to have a good time, to acquire self-realization and self-fulfillment, etc., not precisely injunctions to AVOID the excessive *jouissance*, to find a kind of homeostatic balance?" (Žižek 2007). American personal wisdoms, which are littered across department stores, casually printed onto bubble gum and cough drop wrappings, printed in exotic form onto coffee sleeves, and so on, all indicate to us that there is an attempt to avoid the excessive *jouissance* which intrudes into and indeed eclipses the social bond. Without *the* name-of-the-father, there are only imaginary *names of the father* which are inadequate substitutes that paradoxically produce the subject's spiral into further suffering at the level of *jouissance*.

Similar personal wisdoms and life lessons are littered across the social media walls of our friends, colleagues, and family. The truth is revealed here in a peculiar form: symbolic inscriptions are often transformed in real-time into rectangular images. It seems to me that this demonstrates a new perspective on what Fredric Jameson famously described as the "new depthlessness" within American society (Jameson 1991: 6, 9). Jameson named this the American aesthetic of "postmodernism" and compared the diamond dust shoes of Andy Warhol to the peasant shoes of Vincent Van Gogh. It seems to me that psychoanalytic theory helps to develop these insights in an exciting new direction by demonstrating that postmodernism is not simply an aesthetic or ideology but more fundamentally a discourse, which means, even more precisely, that it is a peculiar solution to the problem of sexuality or death within the capitalist and pragmatic form of social bond.

On social media today, and this is particularly the case on Facebook, user's inputted text—once capable of being copied, pasted, and therefore internally manipulated (because it retained the font in its "symbolic" dimension)—today becomes flattened by the image, reducing or ironing out its inherent symbolic depth. For example, "I am having fun!," can be written on Facebook and instantly transformed into a large rectangular image with a rainbow background. This possibility is not exclusive to Facebook. Other users of various social media platforms are encouraged to curate large collections of personal wisdoms (see Anon 2018a, b; also see the example below from Pinterest). For example, some popular Instagram users produce and curate vast collections of their own personal wisdoms, in image form, and then post them onto their digital wall. Incidentally, each image tends to be signed by the artist, as if it were a beautiful portrait. Indeed, the personal wisdom may be today's American self-portrait. It is as if one is signing a delicate piece of art. The artist seems to recognize that it is through one's art that one makes a name for oneself, and, precisely, it is through the art as a prop that one erects a social link. In every case: the ostensibly symbolic wisdom becomes transmitted and consumed as a work of beauty, a work of art.

This discursive operation is accelerated and revealed in a most blatant way by the well regarded American artist Mark Lombardi. Lombardi's art functions through a strange conflation of image/body and signifier/word. Perhaps it also works in the opposite direction: not only from signifier/word to image/body, but also from image/body to signifier/word. Here, I much prefer the concept of Semblant introduced by Jacques Lacan in his later teaching. Russell Grigg explains that the Semblant "is an object of enjoyment that is both seductive and deceptive. The subject both believes and doesn't believe in semblants but in any case opts for them over the real thing because paradoxically they are a source of satisfaction [...] the semblant fills a lack" (Grigg 2007). I maintain that perverse American wisdom functions through the semblant—which, as Grigg explains, also implies that it functions through a sort of disavowal of the real of castration—so as to avoid the traumatic engagement with the real. Moreover, this helps to explain why Lacan claimed obscurely that "The signifier is the semblant part excellence!" (Lacan 1971). The semblant occurs somewhere in the juncture of imaginary and symbolic, as a perverse solution to the traumatic destitution of castration, of the real. The consequence, as Alain Badiou has put forward in his discussions of the work of Lombardi: "[there is a] substitution of names and bodies [...] we have no picture except for the name" (Badiou 1999).

In one case Lombardi mapped the symbolic network of signifiers linking George W. Bush to Osama Bin Laden. The result was a stunning pictorial map which resembles the geometric properties of a sphere. The imaginary surges forth to function in place of the symbolic, because of a hole in the symbolic itself, and, moreover, because that hole produces, by consequence, an inability to separate from the real: or, rather, the imaginary postures as symbolic axiom.

There are numerous examples of the discourse of American "personal wisdom" that we might point to from American aesthetic culture. These are wisdoms written on the wrappings, or casings, of various commodities (rather than, for example, the kinder surprise egg—which was banned for a long time within America for being dangerous—which includes a little special object inside of it). The move, I maintain, demonstrates also a transition from an "intensional" culture to an "extensional" culture. If the kinder surprise egg had within itself a surprise object to fill the void of its contents, then, American wisdoms are printed on the outside of an object precisely to render that object consistent.

Today's Coca-Cola bottle is a remarkable example of this shift of logic. Slavoj Žižek once taught that Coca-Cola was an exemplary ideological object that concerned "the injunction to enjoy." You *must* enjoy Coca-Cola, and this is elevated into an ideological imperative within capitalism. However, we should go a bit further here: Coca-Cola, exemplary of capitalist discourse, is meant to be shared, as are all commodities. Coca-Cola is best when it is shared, and this has always been one of its central advertising slogans. The bottle of Coca-Cola brings together the family of polar bears for the holiday, so that its function is to establish a social bond, however tenuous.

Such is the latest marketing campaign from Coca-Cola: on each bottle there is a list of proper names: significant people are named, like "Father," "Mother," "Soul-mate," and so on. But there are also more obvious proper names printed onto the bottle such as "Jason," "Sara," and so on. And, finally, various social groups are printed onto the bottles: "Family," "Colleagues," and so on. The most recent addition was to make these stickers that can be removed and placed onto other objects. The point is that there is always another commodity, another Coca-Cola bottle, which may be purchased so as to quickly repair the rupture in the social link. No wonder Francis Fukuyama once claimed that liberal democratic capitalism was the "end of history," and Fredric Jameson claimed that we cannot imagine the end of capitalism: this is the *only* solution on the table to handle the problem of castration. The same point may be made here for cough drops (which, within American, have for a long time included little words of wisdom printed onto each individually wrapped piece) or bubble gum, coffee sleeves, and so on. Thus, there is something a bit more to the writing of names on Starbucks coffee cups than merely satisfying a business requirement for efficiency: we *want* our names on our cups, and we want others to see the names that are on our cups.

Word art, a growing trend within the aesthetics of the American household, has its historical equivalent in the Kitsch knick-knacks which once expressed the simple aphorism that "home is where the heart is." The new American kitsch can be found in the home decor section of any American furniture or retail outlet: "Love every moment, Laugh every day, Live beyond words," "Never stop dreaming," "Smiles, Laughter, and Sometimes Tears," and so on (Wal-Mart 2018). Similar word art pieces may be found at popular book selling franchises. Indeed, the major book chains now dedicate entire shelves to texts whose pages are filled with poems such as the popular ones written by Rupi Kaur. Poetry must now express itself as personal wisdom, and, moreover, it must include a rudimentary sketch or drawing alongside—indeed, within or alongside—the text itself. In every case, we are witnessing the desperate attempt towards the affirmative particular maternal voice.

In *The McDonaldization of Society* (1993), the popular American sociologist George Ritzer famously claimed that sociologists should understand the rationalization processes of McDonalds' Restaurants if they wish to know anything at all about Western modernization. Ritzer is continuing the project set out by the German sociologist Max Weber in attempting to explore and understand the ideal-typical manifestations of instrumental rational social action in the West. Ritzer's project is to think about these instrumental rational types within the context of incessant globalizing tendencies. Ritzer is therefore supplementing or extending the classic work of Max Weber on modernization, rationalization, and social action.

Ritzer is correct in his assertion that McDonalds has become synonymous with American ideology. Indeed, Weber's ideal-typical bureaucratic structure is perhaps best rendered in Ritzer's ideal-typical McDonalds' restaurant. McDonald's restaurants do not therefore only export American food or products, they export, precisely in the structure and function of its internal organization, American ideology. However, we might now look more closely at their aesthetic practices to deepen our analyses: McDonalds' restaurants have begun to incorporate personal wisdoms into their architecture, onto their products (chicken McNugget boxes, fountain soda cups, etc.). At one popular location on the corner of Spadina Avenue and Queen Street in Toronto, Canada, perhaps the most frequented franchise in all of Canada, there is an entire wall dedicated to the dissemination of such wisdom: "Hard work beats talent when talent doesn't work hard," "Life is like a camera, focus on what's important," etc. Fast food, then, with fast ideology; capitalist discourse is nothing but speed—until it burns itself out, until the heart attack.

American wisdom works precisely because it keeps moving. When one piece of wisdom loses its lustre another one is already prepared in advance to replace it, to be purchased, ornamented, and posted on whim as a cheap substitute. Its purpose is always to establish a symbolic moral order that is missing, and yet it can only ever do so in short order. The American too much enjoys the sound of the maternal voice, *lalangue*, as Lacan named it: the popular American app for ordering fast food on one's phone, "tapingo," represents the meaning of "tap and go," and yet, everyday the American enjoys its sound over its meaning: "tah-pang-oh." Žižek, in quite another context, commenting upon the problem of wisdom, voiced the following:

> Whatever you do a wise male [sic] will come and justify it. Like, you do something risky and you succeed, there will be a wise man who will come and say something like […] "only those who risk profit." Lets say you do the same thing and fail, a wise man will come and say "you can not urinate against the wind." This is wisdom, whatever you do a wise guy will come and justify it. (Žižek 2014)

American wisdom does not challenge the ego. It does not disrupt the sense of self. Instead it desires to construct for itself a stable sense of self: Charles Horton Cooley's theory of the "looking-glass self" aims to demonstrate the constitution of subjectivity as such, and not, as it were, the *negation* or *split* of subjectivity. The Lacanian intervention is to demonstrate that the subject is there in the split that occurs after the judgement—and not in the consequent self image that pops out at the end of the chain. American wisdom retroactively affirms the particular circumstance of the subject, in image form. And it provides its solution always faster and faster. American wisdom keeps moving, faster and faster.

And sometimes it burns itself out.

Perverse Discourse and Capitalism

For Lacan, "the capitalist discourse [...] works like clockwork, it cannot work better, but it works too fast, it consumes until it [itself] burns out" (Lacan 1972; my translation). Lacan claimed in his seventeenth seminar that the capitalist marketplace becomes increasingly populated by false objects of desire named "lathouses." Lacan put it in the following way: "[lathouses are] tiny objects that you will encounter when you leave, on the footpath at the corner of every street, behind every window, in the abundance of these objects designed to be the cause of your desire" (Lacan [1969] 2007: 163). Pierre-Gilles Gueguen (2018) went a bit further and claimed that these little objects exist especially within the entertainment market, fabricated as objects of the entertainment industry. Lathouses circulate within a market to fascinate consumers, to captivate them, indeed to capture their eyes. Moreover, they endure only so as to sustain our interest for a short period of time. We see an example of their essential function outlined by none other than Jerry Seinfeld in his award acceptance speech from the 55th annual "Clio" awards:

> In advertising, everything is the way you wish it was. [...] I just want to enjoy the commercial. I want to get the thing. I know the product is going to stink, I know that. Because we live in the world, and we know that everything stinks. We all believe that maybe this one won't stink. [...] But we are happy in that moment between the commercial and the purchase. (Seinfeld 2018)

Seinfeld here describes with clarity the discursive function of the lathouse within advertising, entertainment, or marketing. I want to advance still further by suggesting that these are primarily *aesthetic*—that is, imaginary—objects which are fabricated by industry to "stand in" for the cause of the subject's desire.

Tom Svolos wrote that the lathouses "serve as a stand-in, ready-made object, to take the place of the *objet a* for the subject" (Svolos 2017: 136). Alternatively, they might be understood as "object-props," that is, as dispensable master signifiers (S1s) that constantly slide around within the circuit of various market substitutions. The lathouse is locked into the circuit of the market and yet absolutely dispensable: the subject can easily do away with the lathouse so long as another one is prepared in advance to take its place. The subject exists here torn not between signifiers but rather between commodities, and this produces certain new tensions for the subject (see Samo Tomsic's rigorous study of Capitalism & Lacanian psychoanalysis, 2015).

Imaginary names function as props, as substitutes, doomed to be replaced yet again as the subject moves quickly and surely towards the "next big thing." For some time there was even a popular website titled "The Next Big Thing" which archived short "trending" videos for viewers pleasure. Thus, $, within the formula of capitalist discourse, is meant to represent a fundamental antagonism or rupture for the subject within the social bond. Within any discourse, there is always an impossibility or obstacle to the social link. This is often indicated within Lacan's diagrams by a triangle or double slashes. For example, in the discourse of the university, there is an obstacle in the relation of the master signifier as truth of the discourse and the split subject as the product of the discourse (Fig. 3.1).

However, within capitalist discourse, the non-relation disappears—this is why, perhaps, it must be produced, or, in other words, why the subject often invents solutions that are paradoxically obstacles to his enjoyment. Tomsic writes that the vectors of the capitalist discourse demonstrate that it is grounded "on the foreclosure of the impossibility of totalization that marks [the] other discourses, an impossibility that is structurally determined by the fact that the signifiers constitute an open system of differences" (2015: 220). This is why the sexual non-rapport—or, rather, *sex as such*—is such a problem within capitalist discourse. The antagonism is revealed to the subject very often through the unbearable intrusion of a question concerning sexuality or death. And capitalism serves precisely to obscure the centrality of these questions. Lacan said: "capitalism, [has as its] starting point [...] getting rid of sex" (Lacan 1990: 30).

Fig. 3.1 Jacques Lacan's discourse of the university

$$\frac{\text{Agent}}{\text{Truth}} \quad \begin{matrix}\rightarrow \\ // \end{matrix} \quad \frac{\text{Other}}{\text{Product}}$$

$$\frac{S^2}{S^1} \quad \rightarrow \quad \frac{a}{\$}$$

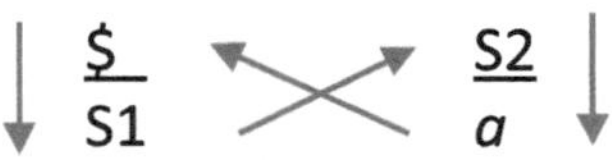

Fig. 3.2 Jacques Lacan's capitalist discourse

Lacan's formula for capitalist discourse appears in Fig. 3.2.

The obstacle of sexual non-rapport has been overcome in capitalist discourse only to produce an even worse problem for the subject: the endless circulation of master semblants, lathouses, designed to provide an obstacle to the intrusion of enjoyment even while providing the subject with further enjoyment. Levi Bryant has read capitalist discourse in the following way:

> 'You must find ever more exotic and different forms of enjoyment!' However, we'll note that in the position of the product of this discourse we now see *objet a*, or the remainder. In the "Milan Discourse" Lacan claims that the discourse of the capitalist is the most ingenious discourse to date in that it creates something like an "eternal motion machine." For each commodity (S2) the divided subject ($) consumes, he experiences a disappointment ("this is not it!"). He is thus compelled to pursue yet another commodity to fulfill the super-egoic imperative. And so it goes on continuously: nothing is ever enough because no commodity is ever "it". (Bryant 2013)

This explains very well why cell phones have become the ultimate American commodity. The latest cell phones perform the function of discourse stabilization by temporarily mending the social link. If the previous discourses aimed at fixing a rupture in the social link, we might claim that capitalist discourse aims rather at *creating the very possibility of a social link*. Each gadget may be replaced suddenly for the next big thing (the next IPhone model, the next software upgrade, and so on), yet each nonetheless serves the function of interfacing with an Other, or, rather, of constructing this Other in the first place.

Take, for example, the current popularity of "Light Phone." This cutting edge American commodity—its headquarters is in California—is sold at double the price of the many cell phones and yet it performs only two features: text messaging and calls. The Light Phone prohibits users from enjoying social media and other related functions (see Light Phone 2018). Indeed, this is its selling point. Its message: "you shall not enjoy all of the features of your regular smart phone!" In other words, the phone is meant to ease burn out and to prohibit enjoyment: "The Light Phone is your phone away from phone. It's a casual, secondary phone that encourages you to leave behind your smartphone [...] Our original Light Phone is intentionally limited to phone calls and nine speed dials." Does this not imply that the Light Phone is one of capitalism's latest and most innovative solutions to the problem at the heart of its own discourse, burn-out? What the subject is purchasing is a father. Indeed, the father has become a commodity that can be bought and sold on the market. The Light Phone installs a new circuit into capitalist discourse which allows it to continue to function *even after it has burned out.*

I propose to amend the aforementioned formula to draw out some inevitable consequences: $\$ \rightarrow S1 \rightarrow \$$. Within capitalist discourse there is always a return to the starting point: primordial subjective division, $. There is always a return to the question of sexuality and death. The circuit always begins anew. In this case, capitalist discourse compels the subject to enjoy, but then, when the subject feels that this enjoyment is too much, she turns, finally, towards some prohibition, and this prohibition is also integrated into market mechanisms. Not only is the "too much" of enjoyment transmitted through market mechanisms, but, it is also transmitted through the gadgets and apps of daily life in America. Tinder is but one notable example. Many further examples abound: for example, at a Conference in California among the tenured class of America's Ivy League professors, I witnessed numerous sessions dedicated to instructing professors on how to keep enjoyment at bay. Workshops concerned themes of how to minimize distractions so as to complete major research papers. During one such session, numerous academics shared their "app preferences" for temporarily silencing social media. It was here that I discovered the apps "Freedom" and "Self-Control:" apps designed precisely to block out, for a limited time, social media, and other computer programs, so that its users can just get some work finished.

When I first moved to America I visited a family owned furniture store to purchase a new mattress. To my surprise, the gentleman who owned the shop immediately guessed the precise type and size of mattress that I required. How could he have known? He told me that he learned to ascertain appropriate mattress sizes according to a simple demographic marker: age. For example, young adults prefer to buy smaller mattress sizes (twin, small double/full size mattresses). On the one hand, these mattresses are more affordable than the luxury sized mattresses. On the other hand, he reasoned that there must be an unconscious motivation involved in this trend: after so many years of relative confinement within the parents' home these individuals are now out in the world for the first time. They desire smaller mattress sizes, then, because this forces intimacy among partners. In a word, young adults desire smaller sized mattresses because they want to bring into existence a sexual relationship. At least, this is the classical Freudian formulation of the problem.

The gentleman continued: middle-aged couples tend to desire larger mattresses. Menopause significantly disrupts the sexual life of the couple, and so, during this time, the couple opts for comfort and for more room between bodies. What they desire is to put the sexual relationship at a distance. Finally, the elderly prefer smaller, single- or twin-sized mattresses in order to accommodate their new circumstances: the sexual or romantic partner has either moved into their own bed or else has passed away. The bed should be structured so as to permit the body to easily roll off before standing up to face the day.

Although I was impressed by this little narrative I nonetheless found fault with it. The claim that young adults desire smaller mattresses did not match with my understanding of capitalist dynamics, where sex sells, where sexuality functions as if one's sexual object choice was a commodity on a supermarket shelf. As it happens, young adults are purchasing larger—queen or king size, even "California King Size"—mattresses (Suckling 2016). The larger mattress is meant to put some distance or some rest to the "too-muchness" of contemporary sexuality. Everyday life involves too much stimulation, there are too many connections, too much information, too many options for intimacy, and so on.

Lacanian clinicians have noted that this is also the discursive structure found among those who suffer from addictions. Increasingly, clinicians are referring to cases of "sex addiction." There are proposals for clinical studies of "hypersexuality," and there is a question of the relationship of sexual addictions to drug addictions (see PsychologyToday 2018). Addiction is not only an epidemic within America, it is probably what is most American about America. Žižek wrote that "the norm in contemporary permissive-hedonist capitalism [is to] surrender to unconstrained consummation whose exemplary cases are drug addiction and alcoholism" (Žižek 2017). These are discourses of enjoyment, or, to use the Lacanian concept, they are discourses of *jouissance*, which explain why in capitalist discourse it is *objet petit a* that is ultimately produced (because the objet petit a is the object cause of our desire).

Similarly, American social media is often understood as a perverse addiction because it encourages the perpetuation of a type of social link founded upon the eternal return of despair. As a demonstration of this see the popular British television series *Black Mirror* (2011–2017). In Season 3, Episode 1, titled "Nosedive," there is a woman who continuously posts images of herself onto various social media channels in order to solicit favourable ratings as a result of these interactions (here, again, we see the imaginary soliciting a symbolic tether). Eventually, she burns herself out from trying endlessly to "fit in" to the social bond. Paradoxically, she found liberation at the end of the episode, but only from within the bars of a prison cell. Inside the four walls of the prison, she found herself permitted to experience her subjective destitution and to make use of it as the rudimentary element for the construction of an entirely novel social link. This time it is a social link founded upon destitution, upon the disruption of the social link itself:What the fuck are you looking at? Just what I was wondering.

Well Don't! Don't? Don't wonder? Uh-huh.
It would be a dull world without wonder.
I don't give a shit about your world.
I don't like your brassiere.
I don't like your moustache.
I don't like your aura.
- My aura? - Yeah.
I don't like your head.
Your entire head is just ridiculous to me.
Really? You look like an alcoholic former weatherman.
You sound like a lost little lamb that just got told there's
no Santa Claus.
What sort of cartoon character did your mum have to fuck to brew
you up in the womb? At least I look like I was born, not shit out by
some tormented cow creature in an underground lab.
You got tossed out of that lab.
- Oh, yeah? - Oh, yeah, flushed out.
- Ooh! - In the trash! - Your face is a fucking - Fucking.
Fucking biological car crash that made Picasso screw his eyes up and
say, "Well, that just don't make sense."
[laughs] - You're a fucking asshole.
- Fuck you! - Fuck you next Wednesday.
- Fuck you for Christmas! - Fuck you! - Fuck you!
[end]

One cannot help but compare this to Plato's infamous allegory of the cave. I shall provide a summary of the allegory from Wikipedia:

> Plato has Socrates describe a gathering of people who have lived chained to the wall of a cave all of their lives, facing a blank wall. These people watch shadows projected on the wall from things passing in front of a fire behind them, and they begin to give names to these shadows. The shadows are as close as the prisoners get to viewing reality. He then explains how the philosopher is like a prisoner who is freed from the cave and comes to understand that the shadows on the wall do not make up reality at all, for he can perceive the true form of reality rather than the mere shadows seen by the prisoners.

This allegory positions the philosopher as the enlightened individual, free from confinement, free from the prison cell. I would like to provide a counterpoint to this allegory. There is a similar allegory from the Quran—Surah 18, *al-Kahf,* translated into English as "The Cave"—also found in the Christian Bible, which tells of seven individuals who abandoned the jouissance of the pagan city to pursue their more dogmatic religious convictions. They take refuge in a cave, and bring a dog along with them to guard its entrance. What we find in this case is quite the opposite from the philosopher's cave: liberation, in this latter case, is found not by moving *outside* of the cave, but rather by moving *inside* of the cave. Indeed, the Quran indicates that the sleepers were most awake precisely when they entered the cave and fell asleep: in the Quran it was written that "you would have thought them awake, while they were asleep."

There have been many variations of Plato's allegory of the cave. For example, McKenzie Wark once amended the allegory by claiming that when the individual leaves the cave he finds himself inside yet another cave, and so on (see Wark 2018). This would imply that there are caves all the way, or, to provide a nice Lacanian twist, it implies that the cave is structured like a Klein bottle so that they only way "outside" of the cave is to move further "inside" and the only way "inside" the cave is to move "outside" of it. This is how I read Louis Althusser's popular claim that the only way "outside" of ideology is to move "inside" of it, and that those who claim to be "outside" of ideology are by definition inside of it (Althusser 1968). In Plato's version we are expected to believe that the people inside the cave are imprisoned by ideology and that there is a place of pure freedom located somewhere outside of the cave. This place of freedom has been criticized by many contemporary theorists, since, for them, there is "no uncontaminated point of departure" outside of power or social structure (Newman 2001). We therefore need within radical theory an alternative to this "uncontaminated point of departure."

The Quranic version begins already within the space of freedom, already within a space of permissive enjoyment: we are confronted with the traumatic freedom of belief, that is, the freedom to worship false idols, images of god, and so on. It is from within this terrifying space of freedom that the "woke" flee into the cave of ideology and go to sleep. What the Quran narrates, then, is the possibility of a flight from *jouissance* whereby our dreams are literally turned against the terrible freedoms of the real. The lesson is instructive: if the so-called Western Platonic vision is one of achieving absolute freedom from the prison of ideology—it is a desire to move beyond the prohibition of enjoyment—then the Islamic vision is one of burrowing within ideology in order to escape the traumatizing abyss of absolute *jouissance*.

I want to return to the question I asked previously: why does the circuit of American wisdom continue to repeat itself if it nonetheless produces the same devastation for the subject? Lacan claimed that the clinical structure of perversion remains suspended within a moment of indecision vis-a-vis the name-of-the-father as master signifier. The subjective operation is one of disavowal: "I know very well, but …" For example, who among us does not already *know very well* that Facebook cashes in on our addiction? Despite this knowledge, many of us continue to use Facebook as a social link (for more on this see Jodi Dean's fascinating *Blog Theory*, 2010). In other words, Facebook functions through the logic of disavowal: the subject knows very well that subjective destitution is the natural consequence of becoming captured within Facebook's circuitry of posts and clicks, but the subject refuses to change the consequent practice of acting as if this knowledge mattered. There is a separation of practice and knowledge, of acting and knowing. This separation poses considerable problems for clinicians who intend to treat perverse addiction. Yet, we are in an even worse situation because perversion has itself been disavowed as a clinical structure (e.g., the analyst now proclaims: "I know very well that perversion still exists, but I act as if it does not exist within my clinical practice"). As Rik Loose has put it: "[…] the [perverse] subject sometimes acknowledges the lack [of subjective destitution] and at other times refuses this [knowledge]" (2002: 276; also see Benvenuto 2016).

References

Althusser, Louis. 1968. Lenin and Philosophy. *Marxists.org*. As Retrieved on November 3, 2018 from https://www.marxists.org/reference/archive/althusser/1968/lenin-philosophy.htm.

Anon. 2018a. Grey's Anatomy Words of Wisdom. As Retrieved on June 14, 2018 from https://www.pinterest.ca/lensuj/greys-anatomy-words-of-wisdom/.

Anon. 2018b. 11 Vital Life Lessons We Learned From 'Grey's Anatomy'. *Self*, July 5, 2016. As Retrieved on June 14, 2018 from https://www.self.com/gallery/11-vital-life-lessons-we-learned-from-greys-anatomy.

Badiou, Alain. 1999. Fifteen Theses on Contemporary Art. *Lacanian Ink*, Vol. 23. As Retrieved on June 14, 2018 from http://www.lacan.com/frameXXIII7.htm.

Benvenuto, Sergio. 2016. *What Are Perversions? Sexuality, Ethics, Psychoanalysis.* London: Karnac Books.

Bryant, Levi. 2013. The Discourse of the Capitalist and the New Symptom [Blog]. *Larval Subjects*, February 11, 2013. As Retrieved on July 26, 2018 from https://larvalsubjects.wordpress.com/2013/02/11/the-discourse-of-the-capitalist-and-the-new-symptom/.

Dean, Jodi. 2010. *Blog Theory: Feedback and Capture in the Circuits of Drive.* Cambridge: Polity Books.

Grigg, Russell. 2007. The Concept of Semblant in Lacan's Teaching. *Lacan.com*. As Retrieved on October 30, 2018 from http://www.lacan.com/griggblog.html.

Gueguen, Pierre-Gilles. 2018. Don't Blame It on New York! *LacanianInk*. As Retrieved on July 26, 2018 from http://www.lacan.com/essays/?page_id=390.

Jameson, Fredric. 1991. *Postmodernism, or, The Cultural Logic of Late Capitalism.* Durham: Duke University Press.

Lacan, Jacques. 1971. Lituraterre. In *Autres Ecrits*, ed. Jacques-Alain Miller. Paris: Seuil.

Lacan, Jacques. 1972. Du Discours Psychoanalytique. In *Lacan in Italia, 1953–1978*, ed. G.B. Contri, 32–55. Milan: La Salamandra.

Lacan, Jacques. 1990. *Television: A Challenge to the Psychoanalytic Establishment*, trans. Joan Copjec and ed. Denis Hollier, Rosalind Krauss, Annette Michelson, and Jeffrey Mehlmen. New York, NY: W. W. Norton.

Lacan, Jacques. [1969] 2007. *The Seminar of Jacques Lacan, Book XVII: The Other Side of Psychoanalysis*, trans. Russell Grigg and ed. Jacques-Alain Miller. New York, NY: W. W. Norton.

Light Phone. 2018. Light Phone. As Retrieved on June 25, 2018 from https://www.thelightphone.com/.

Loose, Rik. 2002. A Lacanian Approach to Clinical Diagnosis and Addiction. In *Lacan and Science*, ed. Jason Glynos and Yannis Stavrakakis. London: Karnac Books.

Newman, Saul. 2001. *From Bakunin to Lacan*. Lanham: R. M. Littlefield.
PsychologyToday. 2018. Hypersexuality. *PsychologyToday.com Definitions*. As Retrieved on November 3, 2018 from https://www.psychologytoday.com/us/conditions/hypersexuality-sex-addiction.
Ritzer, George. 1993. *The McDonaldization of Society*. Thousand Oaks: Sage.
Rousselle, Duane. 2013. The New Hysterical Question. In *Umbr(a): The Object*, ed. Joan Copjec, 71–88. New York: The Center for the Study of Psychoanalysis and Culture.
Seinfeld, Jerry. 2018. Jerry Seinfeld's Clio Acceptance Speech. As Retrieved on November 3, 2018 from https://www.youtube.com/watch?v=uHWX4pG0FNY.
Suckling, Lee. 2016. How Have Bed Sizes Changed Throughout the Ages? *Stuff*. As Retrieved on October 26, 2018 from https://www.stuff.co.nz/life-style/well-good/teach-me/86945440/how-have-bed-sizes-changed-throughout-the-ages-why-has-the-double-died.
Svolos, Thomas. 2017. *Twenty-First Century Psychoanalysis*. London: Karnac Books.
Tomsic, Samo. 2015. *The Capitalist Unconscious*. Brooklyn, New York: Verso Books.
Wal-Mart. 2018. Home Decor. As Retrieved on June 14, 2018 from https://www.walmart.ca/search/word%20art/N-105.
Wark, McKenzie. 2018. *Gamer Theory Version 2.0*. As Retrieved on November 3, 2018 from http://futureofthebook.org/gamertheory2.0/.
Žižek, Slavoj. 1999. You May! *London Review of Books* 21 (6): 3–6.
Žižek, Slavoj. 2007. Do We Still Live in a World? *Lacan.com*. As Retrieved on October 29, 2018 from http://www.lacan.com/zizrattlesnakeshake.html.
Žižek, Slavoj. 2014. Interview in Copenhagen [Video]. As Retrieved on June 7, 2018 from https://www.youtube.com/watch?v=tKoGQpEkpO0.
Žižek, Slavoj. 2017. Can One Exit the Capitalist's Discourse Without Becoming a Saint? *Crisis & Critique* 3 (1): 481–499.

CHAPTER 4

Early American Sociology

Abstract George Herbert Mead, Charles Horton Cooley, and Erving Goffman are central figures within American sociology. In this chapter, Rousselle explores the structure of their sociological discourse to reveal its pragmatist, and hence capitalist, roots. In each case, there is a replacement of the symbolic injunction of the father with the maternal affirmations of the mother. Or, in other words, there is a fall of the symbolic function and a subsequent rise of the imaginary.

Keywords George Herbert Mead · Charles Horton Cooley · Erving Goffman · Symbolic interactionism · Mirror stage · Looking-glass self · Dramaturgical analysis · Frame theory · Sigmund Freud

George Herbert Mead

The ethos of early American sociology forbade psychoanalytic discourse. These scholars were immersed in the ideas of philosophical pragmatism and worked alongside such luminaries as William James and John Dewey. They were also steeped in the psychological teachings of Wilhelm Wundt, whose work G. Stanley Hall introduced into the American academy well before he introduced Freud. Many of these sociologists were later brought under the banner of "symbolic interactionism" by another

D. Rousselle, *Jacques Lacan and American Sociology*,
The Palgrave Lacan Series,
https://doi.org/10.1007/978-3-030-19726-1_4

American sociologist named Herbert Blumer (see Blumer 1963). Blumer described the project of symbolic interactionism in the following way: first, there is a presumption that "human beings act toward things on the basis of the meanings that things have for them," second, meaning arises from social interaction among human beings, and; third, meanings are always implicated in interpretative processes (Blumer 1986: 2). The question of the relationship of symbolic interactionism with psychoanalysis cannot be resolved in this essay, but I want nonetheless to begin to address it.

Herbert Blumer was influential in developing and promoting the work of George Herbert Mead (1863–1931), Charles Horton Cooley (1864–1929), and others. He focused especially on their theories of the "social self" and the "significant symbol." In some sense, the early school of symbolic interactionism became synonymous with early American sociology. George Ritzer, a foremost American sociologist, has claimed that "symbolic interactionism came [...] to dominate American sociology in the 1920s and early 1930s" (Ritzer 2008: 31). Symbolic Interactionism still holds considerable influence within sociology departments across the continent, and it is possible that it has remained the dominant paradigm of American sociology (if only because it has influenced cognate fields).

The popularity of symbolic interactionism is evident within the foremost professional sociological organization, the American Sociological Association (ASA). The Society for the Study of Symbolic Interaction (SSSI) meets at each conference of the ASA and maintains an active research journal titled *Symbolic Interaction*. The project of symbolic interactionism is described by the editors of that journal in the following way:

> Symbolic interactionism, the society's theoretical foundation, is derived from American pragmatism and particularly from the work of George Herbert Mead, who argued that people's selves are social products, but that these selves are also purposive and creative. (SSSI 2018)

It is possible to locate similarities among Freudian/Lacanian psychoanalytic theory and the theories of the early symbolic interactionists. For example, the Freudian "ego-ideal"—which refers to the image one has of oneself when viewed from some external vantage point—is synonymous with Mead's notion of the "Me." Indeed, it is seldom acknowledged that

Mead sought to relate his social theory of the "Me" to Freudian doctrine. He wrote, "[i]f we use a Freudian expression, the 'Me' is in a certain sense a censor" (Mead 1934). We should ask ourselves why Mead decided to relate his concept of the "Me" to the Freudian concept of the "censor" and not to the aforementioned Freudian "ego-ideal," or why he chose to relate the "Me" to the Freudian doctrine at all if he planned to do so in such a superficial and oddly selective manner.

Mead wrote that "the 'Me' is the organized set of attitudes of others which one himself [sic] assumes" (1934). It was Jacques Lacan who made an interpretive cut within Freud's work by drawing out the consequences of a split within the ego among the "ideal-ego" and the "ego-ideal": the ego-ideal was to some extent within the domain of the "symbolic" mental agency because it was the "imaginary" sense of self that the subject assumes for oneself from the vantage point of the "big Other." On the other hand, the ideal-ego was to a considerable extent more firmly situated within the "imaginary." The discovery of a distinction in Freud's writings on the "ideal-ego" and "ego-ideal" was one of Lacan's first major interventions in the Freudian field, and it occurred in his first major seminar (see Lacan [1953] 1991: 129–142). During that initial Serge Leclaire argued that Freud eventually made a change in his presentation of the Ego. Lacan responded: "Exactly. And Freud makes use there of the *Ichideal* [ego-ideal], which is precisely symmetrical and opposed to the *Idealich* [ideal-ego]. It's the sign that Freud is here designating two different functions" (Lacan [1953] 1991: 133). Lacan continued: "one is on the plane of the imaginary, and the other is on the plane of the symbolic—since the demand of the *ichideal* [ego-ideal] takes up its place *within* the totality of demands of the law" (Lacan [1953] 1991: 134). What Lacan said next about the ego-ideal is very important: "Freud [...] identifies it with censorship" (Lacan [1953] 1991: 135).

George Herbert Mead's central contribution, which is, arguably, his social theory of the "Me," was a much less developed and poorly articulated alternative to the Freudian theory of the "ego-ideal." It missed entirely the distinctions and various "knottings" later made by Jacques Lacan among the "imaginary," "symbolic," and "real" agencies. These were concepts that Lacan discovered to be always latent in Freud's work but not expressed as such; it was by expressing them as such that we unlock some of the doors for the Freudian discovery. In some respects, they are very useful alternatives to the other post-Freudian notions, still immensely popular within America, of the "Id," "Ego," and "Super-ego."

Relatedly, Mead missed the importance that Freud placed on the law, and, more particularly, on the law of the father; or, put differently, Mead missed the importance placed on the function of the father within Freudian psychoanalytic theory. Had Mead engaged in Freudian doctrine with the attention of Lacan he would have noticed an odd conflation of "Me" and "imaginary." He would have also noticed the way in which his theory supplanted the symbolic agency of the *Name-of-the-Father* as law, while disavowing its function. The symbolic order is here both "censor" and guarantor of the imaginary sense of self—but it could only offer the latter because of the former function. To my knowledge, Mead allowed himself access to only one of the popular Freudian concepts: the "censor." He picked only what he needed from the Freudian toolbox, only what he needed to gain additional credibility for his theory (in this case, a single concept from Freud's most popular work at the time, *The Interpretation of Dreams*, 1899) and opted to not follow the Freudian insight any further. Like most American sociologists, he chose to relate his work to the Freudian discovery in order to gain legitimacy, even while rejecting the Freudian discovery in practice.

On the other hand, Mead's related concept of the "I" was described with the following two components: first, the "I" is not a "Me" and can never become a "Me"; and, second, the "I" is a response of the organism to the attitudes of others [that is, to the "Me"] (Mead 1934). If, in the first case, Mead neglected the Freudian discovery of "symbolic" agencies by focusing only on the "imaginary" agencies, then, in the second case, he neglected the possibility that the "I" was related to a *real* agency. Admittedly, the concept of the "real" was developed many decades later by Lacan, but it nonetheless was already present in the details of key works from Freud (especially in *Beyond the Pleasure Principle*). The most popular example of the real within Freudian theory was in his book *The Interpretation of Dreams*, in which there is always also the "navel" of the dream. The navel of the dream is that portion of the dream-work that exists beyond any meaningful interpretation:

> There is often a passage in even the most thoroughly interpreted dream which has to be left obscure; this is because we become aware during the work of interpretation that at that point there is a tangle of dream-thoughts which cannot be unraveled and which moreover adds nothing to our knowledge of the content of the dream. This is the dream's navel, the spot where it reaches down into the unknown. (Freud 1899: 525)

The real was already conceived in the work of Freud but its theoretical and practical consequences were seldom drawn by those who only dabbled. The real is that hard kernel of the dream that exists beyond interpretation, beyond the latent and manifest content, it is the "navel" of the dream. But it is also the radical libidinal stratum of the organism which resists absolutely any symbolic or imaginary determinations. However, as Lacan indicated in his 19th seminar, the real is produced as a necessity within and by discourse: "I propose to define [it] as what is produced by the necessity of a discourse. [...] The real is affirmed in the impasses [...]" (Lacan 2018: 29). The real was perhaps even there in a more naïve form during Freud's early theories, as the remnant of the "things" existing outside of the mental apparatus (see Rousselle 2013), as the various versions of the "reality" principle.

The real is one of Lacan's most misunderstood and elusive terms precisely because it describes the elusiveness beyond discourse, language, and image. Lacan put it in no uncertain terms: "the real is that which resists symbolization absolutely" (Lacan [1953] 1991: 66). On another occasion he warned his students to "be wary of the image." The real is the only agency of the tripartite structure of "Symbolic," "Imaginary," and "Real" that is not at all conditioned by or incorporated into Mead's conversations of "gestures," which are supposed to be the primordial ingredients of social interaction. Indeed, the real operates through its very resistance to these gestures hitting their mark within the social link. Mead, working through theories from Wilhelm Wundt, claimed that human beings are to be distinguished from other animals because they can imagine the significant meanings of various gestures within the Other's mind. Human beings are capable of anticipating responses from the Other, and, indeed, of bringing those responses from the Other into being. What makes a gesture truly "significant"—note that "significant" is another word for "signify" or "signification," through the Latin *significantem*, for "meaning"—is the ability to "arouse in the individual making [the gesture] the same responses which they explicitly arouse, or are supposed to arouse, in other individuals" (Mead 1934: 47). Thus, we can feel what the Other feels, and come to therefore have a bond with the other precisely through significant symbols.

I want to take a moment to break down the theory of gestures. The gesture begins, according to Mead, through the voice. Thus, a gesture is another word for what Ferdinand de Saussure or Jacques Lacan named a "signifier." Initially this first signifier is without meaning, without signification, or, to use the Saussurean expression: it is without a mental "concept." It is only a "significant" gesture when the social link is established with the Other, at which point we have what Saussure named a "sign," or what Lacan claimed to be a retroactive tying of signifiers into an imaginary meaning. The subject is constituted—or, if you like, "mind" is constituted—only through this hooking around the Other through signification. No doubt, this is why Mead argued that a vocal gesture must turn or loop back in upon itself so that one can in a sense speak and hear at the same time. Mead wrote:

> It is by means of reflexiveness — the turning back of the experience of the individual upon himself — that the whole social process is thus brought into the experience of the individuals involved in it; it is by such means, which enable the individual to take the attitude of the other toward himself, that the individual is able consciously to adjust himself to that process, and to modify the resultant of that process in any given social act in terms of his adjustment to it. Reflexiveness, then, is the essential condition, within the social process, for the development of mind. (Mead 1934: 132–134)

It is the "I" as real that constitutes the "cut" in the social bond: it cuts into the social fabric of the Other, it cuts into the social fabric of the "generalized other," or, finally, it cuts into the "Me." The problem is that Mead did not adequately explore the implications of the "I" for sociology, and he was not able to extend its function into other domains of mental or social life in the same way that Lacan did through his "return to Freud."

The importance of these gestures for the establishment of a social bond has nowhere been more obvious for me than in my assessment of casual everyday exchanges between individuals within Canada and within the United States. Within Canada, for example, when one bumps into another person on the street there is an iteration of apologies. Or, to take another example, when an individual wishes to cross a highway on foot, a driver will stop his car in the middle of the street and motion for the individual to cross. The individual will resist this gesture, and then insist that the driver continue along his journey uninterrupted. The driver will then insist once again, and the individual will reluctantly cross the street. It is only after this series of exchanges that both parties can continue their day *but now with a sustained reflection on how unsettling was the entire interaction.* It is in this way that the social link is made. In the United States midwest something different seems to occur: when one bumps into another person on the street there is an instant apology, with the returned statement "No, you're fine." Canadians, in my example, seem to use kindness as a front for a social bond based around antagonism with the Other, while Americans use kindness as a quick and dirty solution to engagement with the Other. For Americans, the social bond dissolves very quickly, it is a fleeting experience, and for Canadians the social bond is sustained through neurotic antagonism vis-à-vis the Other.

There is also a similarity among Mead's concept of the "Generalized Other," which is, roughly speaking, an internalized repository of social values, and Jacques Lacan's more obtuse notion of the "big Other." If the Meadian notion of the "I" could have been advanced to account for the agency of the real, then, similarly, the Meadian notion of the "generalized other" could have been explored at some point in its relation to the Lacanian "big Other." The problem was that Mead flattened out the Other (the "generalized other") by placing it squarely within the imaginary: it refers to the imaginary semblance of self. Mead wrote that "[t]he organized community or social group [...] gives to the individual his *unity of self* may be called 'the generalized other.' The attitude of the generalized other is the attitude of the whole community" (Mead 1934; emphasis added). The "unity of self" may otherwise be referred to as "consistency of ego," or, "imaginary self-presentation." In psychoanalytic communities this is often referred to as the process of "introjection," a concept coined by Sandor Ferenczi. However, introjection, claimed Lacan, is not an introjection of images but rather of signifiers—it is therefore crucial that one has elaborated a theory of signifiers, a theory of the symbolic. American psychoanalysts, especially those who take up the work of Melanie Klein, refer to the introjection of "objects." Lacan, in his *Ecrits,* claimed that this is a problematic and one-sided view of Freud's process (Lacan 1977: 655). To correct the theory, Lacan claimed that one *projects* images (this is the theory of "projection") and one *introjects* signifiers.

Mead famously dreamed up the following game analogy:

> The fundamental difference between the game and play is that in the latter the child must have the attitude of all of the others involved in that game. The attitudes of the other players which the participant assumes organize into a sort of unit, and it is that organization which controls the response of the individual. The illustration used was of a person playing baseball.

> Each one of his own acts is determined by his assumption of the action of the others who are playing the game. What he does is controlled by his being everyone else on that team, at least in so far as those attitudes affect his own particular response. We get then an "other" which is an organization of the attitudes of those involved in the same process. (Mead 1934)

Symbolic rules (pertaining to the game) become reduced in their function to an excuse for the discovery and production of a fuller sense of self, that is, to the projection of an imaginary ego. What mattered for George Herbert Mead was not that one come to understand the symbolic coordinates of the game—its prohibitive rules (e.g., "thou shall not …"), its "grammar," and so on—but that the imaginary roles of each of the other players be internalized so as to properly "organize" or produce this "unity" embodied in the "social self." Thus, the social self is rendered as an imaginary consistency by Mead.

These are merely two cases wherein Mead mistook the symbolic for the imaginary, two cases wherein he replaced the symbolic function for a sufficient substitute imaginary semblance: the case of the "Me" as "social self" and the case of the "generalized other" as the coherent internalization of societal attitudes. I have pointed to these two cases only because they seem to me to be the most repeated aspects of Mead's theory within sociology courses in America. Put simply, the lesson is this: Mead's pragmatic sociology forbade any symbolic function which could hold his discourse together. No wonder the word "father" appears nowhere in his pioneering *Mind, Self and Society*, while the word "mother" appears time and again: "a child plays at being a mother, at being a teacher, at being a policeman; that is, it is taking different roles" (Mead 1934). These roles may be understood as the circulation of S1s across the imaginary axis of identification—Mead could not here accept the father as an intervention into the sort of roles that the Mother provides for her children. According to Mead, it is only in the later stage of maturity that these "roles" become consolidated into fixed identifications. With luck, they may even achieve a more stable and long-lasting identification (organized into a "unit") for the subject, thereby forming its more mature social self. In a word, the theory of the mother devours most of Mead's theory, and the father never really steps in except as a substitute through the grammatical semblance of rules involved in playing at games.

In fact, for Mead, part of the ordinary development of mental life for children is not to respond to the name-of-the-father but rather to seek out and turn towards a substitutive imaginary paternal function:

> [Children] *make rules on the spot* in order to help themselves out of difficulties. Part of the enjoyment of the game is to get these rules. Now, the rules are the set of responses which a particular attitude calls out. You can demand a certain response in others if you take a certain attitude. These responses are all in yourself as well. (Mead 1934; emphasis added)

It is the ability to make rules on the spot that helps to fabricate a social link. The pragmatic turn toward imaginary rules assists in the production of S1s. In Meadian language, these S1s perform the function of imagined rules which stabilize the child and form the backdrop of all of the child's later demands within discourse: $\$ \rightarrow S1$. It is only after passing through this stage that all of the attitudes of others cohere into a network of signifiers, otherwise referred to as knowledge. This may be formulated in the following way: $\$ \rightarrow S1 \rightarrow S2$. Notably, this is the flow of capitalist discourse. It is not that there are universal rules in the form of prohibitions which the child actively attempts to repress (obsession) and to combat (hysteria) but rather that there are endless props which sustain the setting of our social interactions, of our social bond, with our audience, with the Others that exist within the theatre of our everyday performance of self.

What is most remarkable about capitalist discourse, indeed what is most remarkable about George Herbert Mead's theory, is that it does not at all discuss the social implications of love. How could one of the most central of social relations not at all be discussed during the period of the formation of the school of symbolic interactionism? Jacques Lacan famously said in one of his late seminars that "any discourse that resembles capitalism leaves aside what we will simply call the things of love, my friends" (Lacan 1972). He also claimed that capitalism has as its key project to not only quickly flee from subjective destitution but also to get rid of the obstacles of love and sex: "that's simply capitalism set straight. Back to zero, then, for the issue of sex, since anyway capitalism, that was its starting point: getting rid of sex" (Lacan 1972). Is this not what happens today within the so-called secular West? Tinder, dating agencies, and a culture of happiness/enjoyment, of "cool" careers and jobs, are more important to many Americans today than love and marriage.

At best, the "cool" career (and here I am using the word "cool" in all of its McLuhanian luster), the pursuit of happiness and enjoyment, determines, precisely, our love lives: it is the career and our personal happiness/enjoyment which *must* come first, and *then*, if we are lucky enough, serious love interests can be pursued. If we get married, it is the "prison" of our enjoyment, of our happiness. But we should only get married if it does not seriously pose an obstacle to our enjoyment or to our career.

Does this not demonstrate not only that "arranged marriages" exist in a more nefarious form within so-called Western "secular" American culture but that, moreover, our marriages and love lives are increasingly arranged not by the personal preferences of our close loved ones (e.g., family, father, etc.), but rather by the much more impersonal capitalist market itself? Today our love lives are arranged almost entirely by the market, and more and more we become objects of the obscure algorithms of capitalism: by dating agencies, by dating apps, by our co-workers, and so on. The contingencies, vulnerabilities, and risks associated with sex are a thing of the past. It is the removal of *risk*, that is, of the *obstacle*, that demonstrates the ingenuity of capitalist discourse: it is without the *real* obstacle of the *relationship*.

We could have seen warning signs of the current situation in the work of the early American sociologists. They also did away with the problems of sex and love. Mead wrote:

> In the more or less fantastic psychology of the Freudian group, thinkers are dealing with the sexual life and with self-assertion in its violent form. The normal situation, however, is one which involves a reaction of the individual in a situation which is socially determined, [...] he brings his own responses as an 'I'. (Mead 1934)

The above passage demonstrates that Mead, like many American thinkers and sociologists, believed that Freud dedicated far too much time to sexual life. Indeed, the American sociologists never wanted to address sexual life or psychoanalytic theory in "its violent form." They saw this as a defect of Freudian theory: the agency of the real, of death-drive, of *jouissance*, and so on, were all reasons to avoid a full engagement with psychoanalysis. Thus, they opted for piece-meal psychoanalysis, they opted for psychoanalysis without the real. Yet, the real is precisely what returns, in a strange and troubling form, in the undeveloped theory of the "I." Indeed, the "I" could have been introduced as a site of real sexual obstacle—the violent form—since it was "a response of the organism," it could have been understood as the site of subjective destitution, $. Instead, it withdraws immediately because of prior social identifications registered in the "Me": $\$ \rightarrow S1 \rightarrow S2 \rightarrow a$. In their eagerness to construct a caricature of Freudian psychoanalysis as overly concerned with "biology" these sociologists certainly neglected the real. Yet, Mead, nonetheless invented an "I" which had its support in biology.

Other rudimentary elements of Mead's work may be compared with Lacan's theory, such as, for example, the Meadian "significant symbol" or "gesture" and the Lacanian "unary trait." The theory of the "unary trait" is already apparent in Freud's *Totem and Taboo* (1913), but Lacan advanced further by finding within the unary trait the subject's possible emergence into language, that is, into the world of signifiers. The unary trait is located at the juncture of the symbolic and the imaginary, and it permits the subject to push from the latter towards the former (imaginary → symbolic, rather than symbolic → imaginary). Hewitson (2018) wrote that "Lacan's innovation on Freud's initial insight was to move us beyond thinking of these unary traits as merely imaginary traits, and instead conceive of them as purely formal marks, like those made by the prehistoric cavemen." The Lacanian theory of the unary trait has become very important in recent discussions of subjectivity within psychoanalysis. I have argued elsewhere that the unary trait functions as a compensatory function for the subject after the collapse of the paternal (symbolic) name-of-the-father (Rousselle 2018). This point was made wonderfully by Veronique Voruz: "[the unary trait] punctuate[s] [the] enunciation in its progressive making sense of the real" (Voruz 2004: 290). We can see how the unary trait may be key to understanding the movement of the psychotic subject into the perverse world of language: the unary trait offers the subject a social link on the spot. It now seems as though the unary trait has more to do with the origin of the subject for the signifier: it is not simply that the subject was passive in the first place, but rather that the child actively brings himself into being as a subject through the prohibition of the mother's desire.

Charles Baudelaire, the famous poet and translator of Poe, elaborated with careful artistry the situation of a small boy who witnessed his father dressing: the boy "looked at the arm muscle, the colour tones of the skin tinged with rose and yellow, and the bluish network of veins" (Baudelaire 1964: 8). This is how the father was brought into the world as a social link, as an Other, for the subject. This is how the child became not the *poet* of everyday life but rather the "painter of everyday life."

Mead wrote that:

> [A] gesture […] calls out an appropriate response; in the present case we have a symbol which answers to a meaning in the experience of the first individual and which also calls out that meaning in the second individual. Where the gesture reaches that situation it has become what we call 'language.' It is not a significant symbol and it signifies a certain meaning. (Mead 1934)

The gesture, like the Lacanian "unary trait," strives towards meaning, it strives towards language and the network of signifiers (S2), and it achieves that dignity only, finally, when it has *imagined* the appropriate response in the mind of the other. One has only to add to all of this the following: it succeeds only when it *imagines* a response in the mind of the Other at that place within the Other which the subject finds to be lacking. This is the basis of language, and it is the basis for the establishment of S2 as such: the subject refutes the possibility of a lack in the Other: s(A̶) (signifier of the barred Other). The perverse subject responds by disavowing the lack in the Other and, similarly, by disavowing the lack in himself.

I turn now to the work of Charles Horton Cooley and Erving Goffman.

Charles Horton Cooley and Erving Goffman

There is something obvious about the relationship of Charles Horton Cooley's theory of the "looking-glass self" and the early Lacanian theory of the "mirror stage" (see Cooley 1922; Lacan [1949] 2006). Indeed, because my aim is not to state the obvious, but rather to attempt an intervention, I shall avoid the obvious similarities and focus on more urgent matters concerning the inadequacies of Cooley's work in relation to Lacan's. In both cases, the mirror is used as an analogy for understanding the social formation of the self: put simply, one obtains a sense of self through the perceived judgements of another who acts, analogously, as one's mirror image. What is most peculiar is that even this similarity of Cooley's "Looking-Glass Self" theory and Lacan's "Mirror Stage" theory has not, to my knowledge, been explored by any scholar.

Cooley introduced his theory of the "looking-glass self" in the following way:

> A social self of this sort might be called the reflected or looking-glass self: 'Each to each a looking-glass [...] reflects the other that doth pass.' [...] In imagination we perceive in another's mind some thought of our appearance, manners, aims, deeds, character, friends, and so on, and are variously affected by it. (Cooley 1922: 152)

The looking-glass self is radically imaginary in that it is situated somewhere at the juncture of the imaginary relationship among egos (i.e., "object relations") and its judgements. Lacan's earlier teaching focused on the axes of the *a*-to-*a'* relationship, that is, the specular relationship. Indeed, Lacan claimed that the *a*-to-*a'* relationship fundamentally obscures the unconscious "symbolic relationship" of the subject to the big Other (the "S-to-A" relationship). Cooley was not at all interested in exploring the symbolic unconscious as an independent agency, he did not at all see the symbolic unconscious as foundational for the specular relationship of egos. Indeed, because of this, he was not at all prepared to explore the *real* unconscious—the drives and the navel of the interpretation.

We might follow this logic through to the end: first, against the position of subjective destitution, which is the threat of not knowing the self, we imagine ourselves, according to Cooley, from the perspective of the other; second, we react or respond to a perceived judgement concerning that idea placed inside of the repository of the other's mind; and, third, we proceed to reformulate our sense of self, that is, our ego, in a higher and more consistent or authentic form. This maps into three sub-processes of the internalization of a sense of self: (1) subjective destitution → *imagine*, (2) react → *judgment*, and (3) knowledge → *self*. It is through subjective destitution, or, rather, with subjective destitution as the 'cause' of the circuit, that imagination sets in; next, it is through the reaction of that imagination that one reacts to oneself with a judgement, and; finally, it is from the judgement that some knowledge or self-awareness becomes produced precisely about our self (e.g., who we are in this world, and so on). I shall provide the following example: (1) subjective destitution → imagine myself as a wonderful professor (compensation), (2) react → I perceive students who doubt my abilities, who perhaps think I may be an idiot, and (3) knowledge → I reformulate myself more modestly as a professor who is not so wonderful. Thus, we have the following series of stages in the formation of the social self: (1) imagination, (2) judgement, and (3) self.

Put another way: (1) we *imagine*, in that we imagine our "self" from the perspective of an other—Why?: to overcome a self that is lacking in some respect, a self that has been experienced as tortured or suffering, a self that strives to be more than it can be: that is, to *exist*; (2) we react by responding to some perceived *judgment*—as Cooley put it, it is an "imagined judgement," in that what matters is not whether or not the judgement really exists but rather that it is perceived to be threatening for the subject; and, finally (3) we become our fuller and truer self, in that we constitute for ourselves some knowledge about our self—it is this *knowledge* that provides some compensation during the dark moments of subjectivation. Thus, in the Lacanian algebra these three stages would be written as follows: (1) \$, (2) S1, (3) S2.

Thus, the movement is: \$ → S1 → S2; from *imagination* to *judgment*, and, finally, towards the constitution of a body of *knowledge*. Crucial, here, is that, logically speaking, the judgement comes after the imagination, after the image. This is quite different from the classical Lacanian theory of the image: the image, in Lacan's early teaching, is the retroactive construction of a judgement—the judgement of the name-of-the-father. We can see this most especially in Lacan's seminar on ethics: "[t]he presence of judgement [...] is essential to the structure [of subjectivity]" (Lacan 1960: 240; my translation). No wonder Cooley wrote the following: "[t]he power to make these judgments is intuitive, imaginative, not arrived at by ratiocination, but it is dependent upon experience" (Cooley 1922: 71).

Cooley went on to discuss the imaginary quality of a judgement, which always involves a game of imitation by the subject, and which succeeds (e.g., its "cash value"): "we can tell by the tone of a dog's bark whether he is a biting dog or only a barking dog" (Cooley 1922: 71). Curiously, it is often the dog, as a classical "phobic object," that the child chooses as a stand-in object for the threatening father. This is demonstrated most effectively in Freud's discussion of "Little Hans" (in his "Analysis of a Case of Phobia in a Five-Year Old Boy") where the little boy's fear of horses was exposed as a substitution or displacement not of the mother but of the father's castration function: the little boy's real father did not adequately intervene as a function of castration. A phobic object occurs as an imaginary object which substitutes for a symbolic paternal function (e.g., the dog, the horse, and so on). In any case, for Cooley, the imaginary takes on symbolic significance, it substitutes for symbolic efficacy. A large portion of Cooley's work was devoted to "the case of those arts which imitate the human face and figure," as in painting, illustrating, art and literature, and so on (Cooley 1922: 71). This is curious in that it demonstrates a preference not for the function of castration—and its consequence in the real—but rather for the image, figure, and face of beauty.

The imaginary substitute for symbolic judgement appears nowhere more forcefully than in the Lacanian expression of the "mirror *stage*." The "stage" in the mirror analogy should be understood today not as if it were a *phase* of mental development but rather as a theatrical stage upon which our role and performance is secured. For Cooley, a consistent role is achieved by way of the audience whose gaze the actor feels as a judgement. The work of a later Canadian-American sociologist, Erving Goffman, famously made use of theatre as an analogy for understanding the social construction of "self." Although Goffman's work has many benefits over similar work conducted by Judith Butler, it nonetheless also comes with its fair share of problems.

Take his most famous work, *The Presentation of Self in Everyday Life* (1956). According to Goffman, it is the analogous theatrical stage that helps the actor overcome the traumatic real of subjective destitution. There is for Goffman nothing behind the superficiality of the performance, of the act, of the roles. Put another way, one never takes off the imaginary mask that is used to conceal lack itself: thus, for Goffman, there is no real self beneath the mask or role. When someone says, as my ex-wife often did, "if only you knew the real Duane ...," there is the comforting assumption that Duane is merely putting on a performance and that there is another more authentic self that has been hidden somewhere from the public. Goffman's view is that there is no more authentic self that is hiding behind the mask, rather, there is something even more authentic, precisely, in taking the mask seriously *as mask*. You cannot take off the masks, you cannot stop the performances, but this point has never been adequately explored in any dramatic way by any of the American sociologists. The impossibility of there being anything beneath the mask is the very name that Lacan gave to the *real*, and it is this *real* that makes possible our sustained conviction that the imaginary performance is *reality*. This is why Alenka Zupancic recently wrote: "in this precise sense, [the real] is of ontological relevance: not as an ultimate reality, but as an inherent twist, or stumbling block, of reality" (Zupancic 2017: 3). What Zupancic means here is that the real is not the images you see before you in your everyday life: it is rather the distortion, disruption, confusion that by necessity bleeds into those images of everyday social interaction. Goffman wrote that "the performer can be fully taken in by his own act; he can be sincerely convinced that the impression of reality which he stages is the real reality" (Goffman 1956: 10). When this happens the actor loses the frame—Goffman sometimes referred to this as "down-keying"—and becomes duped by the comfort of the image at the expense of the revelation of the performance as threaded together by a fundamental impossibility.

Goffman provided us with the thread, but he did not pull on it: he distinguished among the *real* and *reality*. The performance—imaginary as it is—is never the *real* reality, it is only an *imagined* reality, but, nonetheless, for that very reason, it appears to us as *more real than the real*. Reality is always this *more-real* than *real* experience, it is always there to keep us from confronting the traumatic real which forms the authentic backdrop of our everyday lives. In this sense, the real is subtractive. Nonetheless, there are moments when belief in the reality of the performance breaks down. These are moments when the real slips into the act: an actor forgets his or her line, the performer trips on stage, the musician vomits, and so on. I have referred to these "slips" as moments of "subjective destitution." These are the moments when the image is revealed in its real foundation. We stop suspending our disbelief in the image, and begin to believe, precisely, in the inadequacy of the act.

Is it not interesting that an audience tends to suspend their disbelief in the performance during those moments when the performance stages itself precisely as artificial? For example, it often amazes me how there are no critical discussions of the unreality of superhero movies, and yet people continue to view them and fall entirely into its imaginary universe. Yet, the realism of a film like *Gravity* (2013) by Alfonso Curon was the subject of critical commentary—"one of the screws floated in the wrong direction," "Sandra Bullock's hair was moving too much in one scene," and so on—because of its apparent inability to suspend our disbelief. What this demonstrates is that the audience requires, quite fundamentally, more artificiality, more virtuality, in order to suspend their disbelief and immerse themselves into the fantasy as if it were a reality as such. Conversely, the audience requires more realist pretensions within film in order to achieve the critical distance required from the film and see as a performance (e.g., Goffman might have named this "up-keying," that is, exposing the frame as *frame*; Goffman 1974). We can therefore understand the power of theatrical performances of antiquity as compared to the power of cinematic performances today.

Goffman discovered moments of "over-identification" or "cynicism" in actors and audience members. He wrote:

> I have suggested two extremes: an individual may be taken in by his own act or be cynical about it. These extremes are [...] a little more than just the ends of a continuum. Each provides the individual with a position which has its own particular securities and defenses, so there will be a tendency for those who have travelled close to one of these poles to complete the voyage. (Goffman 1956: 11)

The voyage is complete only when one recognizes, as Robert Park once put it, that "the word person, in its first meaning, *is a* mask. It is rather a recognition of the fact that everyone is always and everywhere, more or less consciously, playing a role [...] it is our truer self" (Robert Park as quoted by Goffman 1956: 11–12). Goffman repeats here the problem of Mead, while nonetheless making a crucial advancement: judgement is reduced to an imaginary projective function: "when an individual appears before others, he wittingly and unwittingly projects a definition of the situation, of which a conception of himself is an important part" (Goffman 1956: 155). This structuring sense of self, of imaginary ego, becomes the sole support of a judgement, and, moreover, the sole support of any social situation. We might even say that it becomes the sole support of his discourse and social link.

Whereas social interaction is often understood in relation to the imaginary exchange of meaning, Goffman was able to develop a situational or structural analysis that has its principal function as imaginary. Goffman's structuralism, unlike French structuralism, did not have a symbolic dimension, and this is why Goffman was cherished by symbolic interactionists and structuralists alike. Goffman's level of analysis is best revealed in the following passage:

> [W]e often find that the individual may deeply involve his ego in his identification with a particular role, establishment, and group and in his self-conception as someone who does not disrupt social interaction or let down the social units which depend upon that interaction. (Goffman 1956: 156)

Incidentally, there are numerous stories told by sociologists within the academic gossip-mill about Goffman's personality. Rumors and gossip abound about his perverse social behaviour. For example, once at a conference I was told about Goffman slowly removing furniture from a classroom while two people were in dialogue with one another. He did this to witness whether the frame of their social interaction would be disturbed; put psychoanalytically, he did it to attempt to provoke anxiety in the Other. Goffman was actively involved in his own impression management, and found within social theory a conduit for judgements concerning his own self. His attitude was no different from the current attitude of the Canadian actor Jim Carrey. As Carey once put it: "Jim Carrey does not actually exist [...] There is no me. [...] Jim Carrey is an idea my parents gave me. It's like an avatar. These are all the things I am. You are not an actor, or a lawyer. No one is a lawyer. There are lawyers, law is practiced, but no one is a lawyer. There is no one, in fact, there" (Carrey 2018).

References

Baudelaire, Charles. 1964. *The Painter of Modern Life and Other Essays*, trans. and ed. J. Mayne. London: Phaidon Press.

Blumer, Herbert. 1963. Society as Symbolic Interaction. In *Human Behavior and Social Processes*, ed. Arnold Rose, 179–192. Boston: Houghton Mifflin.

Blumer, Herbert. 1986. *Symbolic Interactionism: Perspective and Methods.* Los Angeles: University of California Press.

Carrey, Jim. 2018. There Is No Me. In *The Talks.* As Retrieved on September 2, 2018 from http://the-talks.com/interview/jim-carrey/.

Cooley, Charles H. 1922. *Human Nature and Social Order.* New York: Charles Scribner's Press.

Freud, Sigmund. 1899. *The Interpretation of Dreams.* Leipzig und Wien: Franz Deuticke.

Goffman, Erving. 1956. *The Presentation of Self in Everyday Life.* New York: Random House.

Goffman, Erving. 1974. *Frame Analysis: An Essay on the Organization of Experience.* Boston: Northeastern University Press.

Hewitson, Owen. 2018. Shades of Subjectivity III. *Lacan Online.* As Retrieved on July 14, 2018 from http://www.lacanonline.com/index/2013/07/shades-of-subjectivity-iii/.

Lacan, Jacques. 1960. The Seminar of Jacques Lacan: l'Ethique, 1959–1960. As Retrieved on September 2, 2018 from http://staferla.free.fr/S7/S7%20 L'ETHIQUE.pdf.

Lacan, Jacques. 1972. The Seminar of Jacques Lacan, Book XX (1972–1973). As Retrieved on April 22, 2018 from http://www.valas.fr/IMG/pdf/s20_encore.pdf.

Lacan, Jacques. 1977. *Ecrits: A Selection*, trans. Alan Sheridan and ed. Jacques-Alain Miller. London: Tavistock Publications.

Lacan, Jacques. [1953] 1991. *The Seminar of Jacques Lacan, Book I: Freud's Papers on Technique*, trans. John Forrester and ed. Jacques-Alain Miller. New York: W. W. Norton.

Lacan, Jacques. [1949] 2006. The Mirror Stage as Formative of the I Function. In *Ecrits*, trans. Bruce Fink and ed. Jacques-Alain Miller, 75–81. New York: W. W. Norton.

Lacan, Jacques. 2018. *The Seminar of Jacques Lacan, Book XIX: … Or Worse*, trans. Adrian Price and ed. Jacques-Alain Miller. Cambridge: Polity Books.

Mead, George Herbert. 1934. *Mind, Self and Society: From the Standpoint of a Social Behaviorist*. As Retrieved on June 18, 2018 from http://livros01.livros-gratis.com.br/bu000001.pdf.

Ritzer, George. 2008. *Sociological Theory*, 8th ed. New York, NY: McGraw Hill.

Rousselle, Duane. 2013. The New Hysterical Question. In *Umbr(a): The Object*, ed. Joan Copjec, 71–88. New York: The Center for the Study of Psychoanalysis and Culture.

Rousselle, Duane. 2018. A Portrait of Baudelaire as a 'Man of Genius': Ordinary Psychosis Within the Age of Modernity. *Psychoanalysis Lacan* 3. See http://psychoanalysislacan.com/.

SSSI. 2018. Society Information. As Retrieved on July 13, 2018 from https://onlinelibrary.wiley.com/page/journal/15338665/homepage/society.html.

Voruz, Veronique. 2004. The Topology of the Subject of Law. In *Lacan: Topological Speaking* ed. Ellie Ragland and Dragon Milovanovic, 282–313. New York: Other Press.

Zupancic, Alenka. 2017. *What Is Sex?* Cambridge: MIT Press.

CHAPTER 5

On Strangers

Abstract The stranger is a shadowy figure of American sociology who exists with one foot outside the door of the sociological tradition (as in the case of Georg Simmel) or with both feet firmly outside the line that separates the periphery from the centre (as in the case of ibn Khaldun). In this chapter, the author situates Simmel and ibn Khaldun as strangers within the tradition of American sociology. Rousselle provokes a return to "social geometry" so as to open up a possible move into the sort of topological analysis that Lacan increasingly favoured in his late teaching (a topology of the social bond).

Keywords Georg Simmel · Stranger · Ibn Khaldun · Topology · Social geometry · Asabiyyah · Uncanny

Two Strangers

The "stranger," as a shadowy figure of American sociology, exists either with one foot outside the door of the American sociological tradition (as in the case of Georg Simmel) or (as in the case of ibn Khaldun) with both feet firmly outside the line that separates the periphery from the centre. In this short chapter I would like only to situate Georg Simmel and ibn Khaldun as strangers within the tradition of American sociology. I do not intend to provide an overview of their work, I do not intend

D. Rousselle, *Jacques Lacan and American Sociology*,
The Palgrave Lacan Series,
https://doi.org/10.1007/978-3-030-19726-1_5

to introduce their work more forcefully to American audiences. Rather, I intend to provoke a return and reinvestigation of the topic of "social geometry." It is my conviction that such a return opens up the possibility of a move into the sort of topological analysis that Lacan increasingly favoured in his late teaching (a topology of the social bond). The stranger, as a concept, has a lineage which we might trace within the sociological tradition from ibn Khaldun ("the desert" or "nomadic people"), Georg Simmel ("the stranger"), as well as Sigmund Freud ("the uncanny"). However, it is possible that the Lacanian "stranger" is an altogether different beast.

Within university discourse the stranger becomes reducible to what Jacques Ranciere has named the "non-part," or, as he sometimes has put it: "the part of no part." It has been with some urgency that American sociology has aimed to incorporate the "non-part" precisely by making it a "part" of the American tradition; that is, by preserving within the space of the tradition or the discipline, some "chunk" of knowledge, some theory, or some discussion precisely about the "non-part." The "non-part" is nothing but that excessive kernel of enjoyment that Lacan named *objet petit a*.

For example, George Ritzer, within his popular undergraduate textbook *Sociological Theory*, has, throughout the several dozen iterations or volumes of the text, increasingly incorporated the work of fringe sociological thinkers such as Georg Simmel and ibn Khaldun. Yet, for me, it is a question of how these figures have become incorporated into the tradition. On the one hand, Georg Simmel, through time, has eventually been granted his own chapter alongside three other essential names-of-the-sociological-tradition within the "Classical Theory" section of the text: Karl Marx, Emile Durkheim, Max Weber, and Georg Simmel (with very brief detours into the work of Auguste Comte and others). However, ibn Khaldun has, throughout time, only been afforded a short blurb in one of the opening chapters. We should ask ourselves what accounts for this difference of treatment. To be very clear: it is not my intention to pursue university discourse in such a way as to advocate for complete acceptance and integration of "strangers." Indeed, if there is any basic claim that I am making here it is the following: there is already within American sociological theory a stranger which the tradition simultaneously accepts and rejects.

Does this not indicate that Georg Simmel and ibn Khaldun are strange to the tradition of sociology in two quite different ways? For the moment consider that Georg Simmel seems to occupy the position of "masculine logic" within Jacques Lacan's theory of "sexuation," while ibn Khaldun seems to occupy the position of "feminine logic." Lacan's claim is that the speaking being is cut or disrupted essentially by sex, and this was, for example, why he famously stated that "there is no such thing as a sexual relation": it wasn't because of a barrier *between* man and woman, or, if you like, between American Sociology and Non-American Sociology, but rather it was because of a barrier *within* each independent man and woman.

In spite of this, we can nonetheless claim that man and woman are each in their own independent way reducible to their discursive, logical, or spatial position. Take, for example, Lacan's claim that "all men are subject to castration" or "there is no woman who is not subject to castration." There are two ways to read these formulae within Lacanian circles. There is the more popular position which places the subversive emphasis on the 'not-all' logic of feminine sexuation: woman, in this case, seems closer to the real, and therefore more outside of the symbolic determinations, and this is what grants her a more emancipatory position. However, there is another way to read it offered to us by Slavoj Žižek: "woman is fully caught in the phallic function (nothing of her is outside) while a man only is partially caught in it (the exception to phallic function grounds the male position" (Žižek, n.d.). In this version, we read more carefully the Lacanian formulae of sexuation to reveal its terrifying dimension.

It seems to me that the demand to incorporate Georg Simmel into the American tradition of sociology demonstrates that he is already partially caught up into the phallic function. Indeed, one reviewer of this manuscript demanded that I elaborate on Georg Simmel's work, but why was there no demand to elaborate on ibn Khaldun's work? In any case, this implies, does it not, that Simmel is partially included within the tradition of sociology (in the same way that Freud is only partially included within the tradition of American sociology), and that this inclusion comes with the demand for a coherent and systematic account of his work. Thus, Simmel's work is implicated and determined by the readings that sociologists have given to his work (as in the symbolic interactionist tradition), while, to some extent, his work, like the work of Erving Goffman, continues to resist this gesture of university discourse.

However, what can we say about ibn Khaldun? Again, there was no request or demand made by any reviewer for expansion or elaboration on any of ibn Khaldun's theories. Ibn Khaldun, here, seems to be on the side of feminine logic: for the American tradition of sociology it is as if he does not at all exist. Indeed, Lacan once claimed that for woman's sexuation, that is, on the question of *the* woman (e.g., her symbolic and imaginary identity): "the woman does not exist." Except, as a consequence of this inexistence, ibn Khaldun, through this exclusion, is all the more dominated by the American phallic function. There does not exist a representation of ibn Khaldun's work that does not belong to the American tradition (https://www.youtube.com/watch?v=x4-N2lzTPkk). Indeed, it is for this reason that many non-Western Muslim scholars claim that ibn Khaldun's work is (like much of Sufiism) the only source of engagement for secular Westerners.

We have therefore two strangers. They demonstrate two logical modes of subjection to the phallic function of tradition. In either case, there is a discursive operation irreducible to any university discourse, any capitalist discourse. The attempt to transform Simmel into a coherent object of scholarship will always demonstrate precisely that something is lacking within American interpretations; the attempt to transform Khaldun into a coherent object of scholarship will be performed much more easily. That, precisely, is the American fantasy that Edward Said so attacked: *kahldun will be made a representation of representations.*

Fast food, then, for the American McUniversity.

Georg Simmel

Georg Simmel investigated mental life and the social bond. Yet he was not interested in separating the investigation of the social bond from the investigation of mental life. Rather than conflate the two, he opted to give priority to the problem of the individual in his or her confrontation with the social bond. For example, he wrote in "The Problem of Sociology:"

> [T]he givens of sociology are psychological processes whose immediate reality presents itself first of all under psychological categories. But these psychological categories, although indispensable for the description of the facts, remain outside the purpose of sociological investigation. It is to this end that we direct our study to the objective reality of sociation, a reality which, to be sure, is embodied in psychic processes and can often be described only by means of them. (Simmel 1971: 35)

For Simmel, the individual positions himself in a confrontation against Society, which, given that Society or the Social bond reveals itself in the discursive dimension of the Lacanian Other, can be thought only in terms of the masculine fantasies that render the other in phantasmatic form. Society is here the phantasy of man. In 1975, Lacan stated that "woman is a symptom of man," which, from the standpoint of masculine sexuation reveals that woman can only enter into man's universe as a phantasy projected onto the *objet petit a*. Similarly, for Simmel: Society is a symptom of the individual; a symptom of the individual's inability to establish a social link.

All forms of social life—"social forms," as he named them—are relatable to the problem of distance. It is distance, then, with which all of discourse is predicated, and it is distance which the individual must confront during his constant social interactions. Similarly, for the topologist (an improvement in the history of thinking about mathematical geometry), it is the "hole" that articulates the precise structure of distance. Indeed, there are notable Lacanian psychoanalysts who describe the Freudian unconscious in its "real" dimension (as a 'hole') rather than in its more classical "symbolic" dimension (hence interpretable dimension). In any case, we can claim that the concept of "distance" is threaded throughout the entire works of Georg Simmel (see Ethington 1997; Cooper 2010). I shall suspend this discussion for the moment in order to provide a gentler gateway into Simmel's work, strange as this work may be.

A turning point for sociology occurred during the moment of its academic establishment in France. Positivist philosophy set the tone for much of the academic sociological discussions that occurred in France for some time. Put simply, positivism provided sociologists with the foundational or paradigmatic belief that social science ought to replicate the methodological assumptions of the natural sciences. It was believed by Auguste Comte that sociology would achieve the superior position of all the sciences because of its unique subject matter: society. Emile Durkheim was born into this bold new world as the "Father" of a new discipline of academic sociology—establishing, within the university, the discipline of Sociology that continues to enjoy a nice reputation within many parts of Europe. Durkheim's major project was therefore to "extend scientific rationalism to human conduct within society" (Durkheim 1895).

Durkheim introduced a type of "social realism" into sociology: society, he figured, must be understood as its own independent and autonomous (and thereby "coercive") reality. Durkheim, in no uncertain terms, proclaimed that "God is Society, writ large," without realizing, in that statement, that Society must therefore be the Other. No wonder one of the "social facts" Durkheim wanted to study was language itself. "Social facts" are those independent constraints that force their forms onto social groups/individuals—they are to be studied only in relation to other social facts. An exemplary attempt to demonstrate the power of this new sociological technique was provided in his book *Suicide* (Durkheim 1897). Suicide, which appears at first to be the subject matter of psychologists, can be studied uniquely by sociologists as a social fact. The fact that suicide occurs differently because of relative levels of social integration and regulation demonstrates quite forcefully the power of the sociological method. Thus, for Durkheim: "the whole [society] is greater than the sum of its parts [individuals]." If Durkheim discovered the Other but opted to study the social Other independent of the subject (in the Lacanian sense as that which exists between the signifiers of language, or, rather, "that which is represented by one signifier for another signifier") then Georg Simmel began with a different point of departure. Simmel, like his more famous colleague Max Weber, retained the subject and opted to ask the more pertinent question of how the social link can be established when the Other is missing. The social form (or Weber's equivalent: the "ideal-type") is not therefore an independent symbolic Other that we find in Durkheim's work. It is rather the Other of the social bond fashioned precisely through *verstehen*, through the miracle of the subject's engagement with the world itself. For Simmel society was precisely the object form of the interaction of various individuals: "for unity in the empirical sense of the word is nothing but the interaction of elements" (Simmel 1971: 23).

Thus, if the classical psychoanalytic model posited a symbolic father—the Name-of-the-Father—who, through his universal prohibition ("No!") of enjoyment, produced the subject of language, then, in the latter Lacanian model: the father is no longer in this position. One can do without the name of the Father provided that one makes use of it as a prop: the universal dimension of the Father, as an external, independent, coercive force, is lost in favour of a father who is made up from the bricolage of the subject's chaotic reality. What we see in the difference, then, of the French positivist (Comte, Durkheim, etc.) tradition of sociology and the German anti-positivist one (Simmel, Weber, etc.) is the same move: against the symbolic Other of society (as a social fact) there is the Other of social forms and ideal-types which the subject may make use of to form a more coherent picture of his chaotic social reality.

The problem is currently that people are only just beginning to seriously engage with the work of Georg Simmel within American Anglophone sociology. As a result, suddenly, there are new translations of his work emerging and being discussed in American periodicals. But for a very long time there was no "Georg Simmel" chapter or module within undergraduate sociological theory courses. The case had to be made by many respected sociologists that his work was worth examining. It is in fact quite difficult to consider him a forefather of sociology—indeed, an important "Name-of-the-Father"—because: (1) much of his work has not been available (indeed, is still not available) to English readers, (2) his work did not develop any "grand systems" or "grand theories" (e.g., "Capitalism," "Suicide," "Protestant Work Ethic," and so on), (3) he did not write large sustained investigations ("rigorous studies") of society—quite the opposite, Simmel's most famous pieces are short essays, sometimes of no more than 4–5 pages, (4) much of Simmel's work has been eclipsed by his friend and contemporary Max Weber, and (5) the style of Simmel's engagement is often viewed as erratic and idiosyncratic (it does not continue the academic style of tradition university discourse).

Simmel received his Ph.D. in 1881 but he found himself up against a problem: he could not find an appointment within the university as a professor or researcher. Despite the popularity of his lectures, he nonetheless remained an outsider to the university system, retaining a *privatdozen* (unpaid) position for almost twenty years. And then, after almost two decades, he lost that position. In 1901, Simmel was awarded the honorary title of "Extraordinary Professor," which was a mark of prestige, no doubt, but it certainly didn't help him find financial stability. Although he remained a stranger to the university, he nonetheless continued his research and work alongside the university. He founded, with Max Weber and others, the "German Society for Sociology." It was in 1914 (at the age of 56) that he finally received a paid position as a professor within the university in Strasbourg. However, this appointment was interrupted because of the war. Next, he applied to Heidelberg as a department chair, and his application was rejected. Four years later he died of liver cancer. He was always a stranger, then, and his personal narrative demonstrates the profound social issue of this strangeness in his work.

Simmel developed a sociology of space. A "social geometry," as he called it. Social geometry aimed to discern how variations in numbers and space might change the relationship one has not only to oneself but also the world. I maintain that his short essay on "The Stranger" remains the clearest demonstration of the importance of social geometry for understanding the social bond as discourse or topology. The stranger is a social form of interaction, or, if I may put it like this, a social form of distance. Incidentally, what we learned in his "Quantitative Aspects of the Group" essay is that it is only with the introduction of a third member to the group, or, to be more precise, a third element, that distance can be achieved. This "third" other is always a solution, then, to the problem of the over-proximity of the Other within the dyadic relationship. The third figure is therefore something like a Father, or, as we've seen in his work: the judge. For Freud, the third is often recognized as the super-ego, as an internal split of the One (e.g., the harmony or fusion of the dyadic Mother–Child relationship) into two. It is therefore only the "triad" which can give rise to the number two. We can say that it is only possible to count to two after we have already counted to three.

The stranger, as the third, who is elevated to the *at-least-one* who may have an objective position from which to judge from the position of the law, introduces the possibility of there being secrets and gossip. When the unity of the Mother–Child relationship has been disrupted by the *at-least-one* then it is possible for two elements, two individuals, to share secrets and gossip about the third (father; as my ex-wife, for example, who was the step-mother to my son, often did to bond with my child). Indeed, the sharing of secrets or of gossiping is identified by Simmel as a mode of social bond; and it is precisely a bond that is formed by the desire to return to the presumed (phantasized) harmony of the relationship. It will never be an adequate solution, it remains, therefore, the neurotics solution to make up for the lack of social relationship.

In any case, the stranger is a figure identifiable according to some measure of distance within the interaction of members of society. We might take a brief excursion into set theory (a topic that fascinated Lacan): the stranger, for Simmel, becomes defined in strikingly set theoretical language: "*in* the group but not *of* the group." The "empty set" of set theory belongs to the group/set but is not a member of that group/set. This is no different from the sort of statement one might read from our contemporary Alain Badiou (whose work I shall explore in another chapter) on "belonging" and "inclusion." Simmel opens his stranger essay in the following way:

> [The stranger] is, so to speak, the potential wanderer: although he has not moved on, he has not quite overcome the freedom of coming and going. He is fixed within a particular spatial group, or within a group whose boundaries are similar to spatial boundaries. But his position in this group is determined, essentially, by the fact that he has not belonged to it from the beginning, that he imports qualities into it, which do not and cannot stem from the group itself. (Simmel 1971)

It is important to understand the stranger within the spatial metaphor that Simmel has constructed: he is not an outsider per se but is rather a potential outsider. Lacan invented the concept of *extimacy* to describe this geometrical position. Jacques-Alain Miller writes: "this expression 'extimacy' is necessary in order to escape the common ravings about psychism supposedly located in a bipartition between interior and exterior" (Miller 2008). Miller continues: "if we use the term extimacy in this way, we can consequently make it be equivalent to the unconscious itself. In this sense, the extimacy of the subject is the Other" (Miller 2008). The stranger is therefore Society, in its unconscious dimension, as spoken through the medium of the subject's ego. But Simmel paints a much simpler picture. Imagine that there are people who you do not even know to exist in some *other* country. These people are not strangers because *you know that you do not know them.* Now, imagine that there are people near you at this moment who you can point at, their existence is such that there is a quality that you do not know anything about. These are the strangers who are at the periphery of the social bond: *we do not know what they know about us.* We can point at the stranger and we can be sure that we do not know where they stand, what they see in our social interactions, and so on.

The stranger is therefore simultaneously near and far, close and distant, local and global. He is the "inner enemy," rather than a purely external enemy. Thus, while George W. Bush proclaimed that "you are either with us (inside) or with the terrorists (outside)," Simmel disrupts this simple demarcation of space by exposing an *extimate* dimension in the figure of the stranger. American radicals have therefore offered a nice rebuttal to the Bush establishment by pointing at the various *domestic* terrorists that exist within the American population. Yet, we should be very clear here: there is also something special about being placed in the position of the stranger. Because of his social location the stranger can do things that the non-stranger cannot do: he can write about certain topics, teach in certain ways, and so on. The stranger is both privileged and dangerous, a risk and a potential reward. The stranger is necessarily mobile or nomadic while the insider is fixed or sedentary: he can come and go as he pleases in a way that those who are fixed at the centre of a social bond cannot.

Ibn Khaldun

Ibn Khaldun was an Islamic sociologist born in the 1300s. His work has been influential in Economics, History, Demography, Religious Studies, and, some would say, Sociology. In all cases, I credit him with being among the first (although we might also credit ibn Arabi and many others) to offer a lasting, and arguably still unsurpassable, analysis of the social bond. Yet, within American sociology, it is almost as if he has never existed. Writing out of Northern Africa, but constantly connecting and disconnecting from social bonds along various regions of Tunis, Fez, Granada, and so on, he memorized the Quran at a very early age. Unlike Comte, who constantly tried to distance himself from religion, Khaldun structured his thinking quite explicitly in relation to religious precepts. And probably for a good reason, since, from *religare* (Latin), the word religion implies that its function is "to bind together."

Ibn Khaldun's pivotal work was *The Muqaddimah* (1377). The word "muqaddimah" translates from the Arabic into "opening," "introduction," or "awakening," and is similar, in effect, to "prolegomena." Already we should understand the importance that ibn Khaldun placed on language. Although *The Muqaddimah* is a very long work, it was written, apparently, very quickly. Its central concept is perhaps the Arabic word *'asabiyyah*, which has been translated into various English words including "social solidarity," "civilization," "morality," "urbanism," and so on. I choose often to translate the word simply as "Social bond" or "Social link." Thus, at the centre of ibn Khaldun's work is a key sociological concept.

I believe that ibn Khaldun introduced a very early discursive logic similar to the one opened up in Lacan's late work on sexuation. Thus, whereas ibn Khaldun used the concept of *'asabiyyah* to discuss the social bond, Lacan, for his part, used the word *discourse* to discuss the social bond. For Lacan, discourse was at the centre of the experience of the social bond. Ibn Khaldun lived many centuries before semiotics or discourse studies, but his approach nonetheless demonstrates an understanding of psychoanalytic discourse *avant la lettre*. For ibn Khaldun, there are stronger and weaker forms of *'asabiyyah*, such that the moral order—which, you may recall, for Freud was the superego, or the Father's function—is relatively *stronger* or *weaker*. We might position the Name-of-the-Father here in the centre of the social bond. It is that to which all of social life is directed, as if from the *objet petit a* toward the Phallic centrepiece. When the social bond is stronger then so too is the moral order, and the sedentary population, who live at the centre of the social bond, are fixed in their precise location. Is it any wonder, then, that certain spatial locations are often marks of tremendous sites of power within any social bond (e.g., the "white house," the "Kremlin," and so on).

For Lacan, the Phallus, as the function of symbolic castration, occurs there in the phallocentric model circumscribing masculine sexuation. Yet, for ibn Khaldun, weaker *'asabiyyah* is associated with the nomadic population—what I am tempted to call nomadic or strange "multiplicities"—who live on the periphery of the social bond. For the nomadic population, it is a question of whether or not they "exist" at all. According to the sedentary population, their existence occurs under erasure. From the periphery of phallic discourse there is a feminine form of sexuation which outlines woman who, because of being on the periphery of the moral and social order, nonetheless finds herself *all the more implicated* in the symbolic universe of discourse. So it is the same, for ibn Khaldun, with the nomadic desert people who live on the periphery of the social bond. It is from this periphery location, this strange location, that the outlying multiplicities are capable of binding together a new moral order which may eventually replace the prevailing or existing one. The multiplicities therefore bring themselves into existence from the zone of their inexistence.

A certain distance separates the sedentary population (singular) from the periphery populations (plural). The sedentary population are *at-least-one* to put it in Lacan's language, in that they are situated at the phallic anchoring point of the moral and social order; they are equipped, then, with a semblance of mastery or coherence, of unity, of *oneness*. The nomadic population of tribes are, however, a multiplicity without unity, or, put another way, a multiplicity *in search of unity or existence*, and are thus caught into the deadlock of their own structural division: *a* → Phallus. What, one might ask, of the multiplicities who remain on the periphery after the triumph of the cyclical movement of history whereby the periphery takes centre stage and comes into existence as a semblance of social cohesion? These, I would claim, are the true multiplicities, and without those multiplicities (of multiplicities) there would not be any birth of a truth of the division of the periphery as such.

Thus, ibn Khaldun's cyclical spatial model of changes in the social bond—whereby the nomadic people are preparing for the coming social order, and the prevailing social order crumbles upon its own decadence—seems to operate according to a mobius structure. It is therefore incorrect to claim that ibn Khaldun offers a "cyclical" account of the movement of social change. It is much more correct to posit that ibn Khaldun stumbled onto an understanding of the lack of harmony or relation among the sedentary and the nomadic people: they are, as it were, two sides of the same mobius band: the nomadic people walk a bit along that band and end up in the sedentary position, while the sedentary people walk along that band and end up spit out into the refuse of the *objet a* (nomadic or desert multiplicities). A much more forceful position would have been to examine the internal structural division of each social location.

Thus, there is a disruption inherent to each position: the moral order, precisely because of falling into moral decadence, inevitably declines. Lacan named this "castration anxiety," or the "return of the real." And the periphery multiplicities, precisely because of their desire for moral certainty, inevitably ascend. This is the dynamic of "knavery and foolishness" outlined so often by Lacan: for "knavery," there is no hold on truth, and for "foolishness," there is truth, but it always a spoiled truth. This outlines the political split that occurred both in France and in America—indeed in much of civilization—among the left and the right: knaves and fools.

But ibn Khaldun's similarity to Lacan's work extends much further: he was oriented in "*adab*," which, in the anglophone world of academia means: "letters." The best French word, notes Bruce B. Lawrence in his discussion of ibn Khaldun, is the French "*litterateur*," a person who is knowledgeable and interested in literature, broadly. Lawrence wrote: "[a] litterateur is attentive to words, to their expression in both speech and writing but above all, to their polyvalence. Words can mean many things in different times, places, and contexts. Though this may seem like a truism today, it was far from acceptable knowledge [at that time]" (Lawrence 2005: xi). Thus, ibn Khaldun, like Lacan, recognized the importance of signifiers as nodal points for truth within the discourse of his interlocutor. The analyst recognizes that signifiers (S1) take on singular relationships with the battery of other signifiers (S2) to form the unique linguistic make-up of a subject's discourse. Thus, the word "cat" is related to a different network of signifiers in my lexicon than it would in another's lexicon. This, for Saussure, was the "value" of a signifier: the signifier "cat" takes on value because it is not "bat" or "rat." Indeed, Lawrence pointed out that Khaldun, like a psychoanalyst, would deliberately use a word with a different meaning depending upon his audience (ibid.).

Most interesting is that ibn Khaldun developed a theory, within the social bond, of the interaction of "Events" (*khabar*) and "Tradition" (*hadith*). It is a novel dialectic which does not presume that one or the other is more advantageous (e.g., in the work of Alain Badiou there seems to be a presumption that the "Event" is of much more importance than the repetition of tradition). Indeed, commentators, such as Lawrence, and even Franz Rosenthan, the central translator of the English version of the *Muqaddimah*, decided to capitalize the first letter of each word so as to elevate them to the dignity of concepts. One cannot but be struck by the importance today within sociological theory of the Event (see the chapter in this volume on Alain Badiou's theory of the "Event"). Sociological theories of the Event offer an engagement with the "real," which is a corrective to the disengaging theories of the early American sociologists. In any case, ibn Khaldun believed in the importance and priority of both Event and Tradition. An Event occurs in the first instance of any social bond, always within the *badaah* (desert social group), and this, precisely, "sets the stage for what follows" (Lawrence 2005), which is the emergence of a world civilization (*'umran*) in the form of sedentary or urban civilization.

There is an interplay of Event and Tradition. As Abdallah Laroui writes: "the normative draws its sense solely from itself, while the account, which is indicative, draws its sense both from itself and from an external fact which corresponds to it." How are we to interpret this? The normative position within history, indeed of the prophet Mohammed, becomes self-referential and tautological. But the "account" draws its essence from the Event *as well as* the marks of the tradition which sometimes seek to suture itself off from any Evental occurrence. Thus, whereas for Alain Badiou the Event leaves a "mark" or trace within the world of tradition, for ibn Khaldun there must be within the tradition of the World also an attempt to touch the real Event. The Event must therefore move into the world and leave a mark but the world must also respond with some courage to give an account of the Event in the terms with which it has already been made familiar.

Ibn Khaldun encourages his readers to not blindly repeat Tradition but rather to have the courage to "stand up against the authority of truth." He makes, in his analysis of history, a distinction between "reporters" and "critical thinkers." Reporters, he insists, repeat the truth and pass it on—they "relay" the truth. Critical thinkers, on the other hand, have insight that can sort out the "hidden truth," which is the real touch of the truth: "it takes knowledge to lay truth bare and polish it." Thus, for ibn Khaldun knowledge pre-exists the truth and allows for the fashioning of a real truth which may become the mark of a new truth.

So much for the strangers of sociology. What of the stranger within the Freudian field? The stranger of the Freudian field, is "uncanny." In this version of the stranger there is only a symbolic unconscious awaiting revelation: there is something which at once seems foreign and yet which, upon closer inspection, is *more true to me than I was initially prepared to admit*. There is the fascinating discussion from Freud of his look into a window, seeing a strange man motion past him. It was only later that he came to realize he had caught sight of himself in a reflection. The stranger is therefore an "*unknown knowledge*," somebody who is more familiar to me than I was prepared in the first instance to admit. Yet, is it not the case that Freud, in his essay on the uncanny, places the loss of one's eyes (castration anxiety occurring within the scopic field, within the field of the gaze) at the centre of the experience of the uncanny? Thus, the stranger, in the final instance, is the real which obstructs, limits, and insists, from within the gaze of the Other, the picture that I am. The stranger is therefore what is most avoided within American sociological discourse.

References

Cooper, Robert. 2010. Georg Simmel and the Transmission of Distance. *Journal of Classical Sociology* 10 (1): 69–86.

Durkheim, Emile. 1895. *Rules of Sociological Method*. Paris: Librairie Felix Alcan.

Durkheim, Emile. 1897. *Suicide*. Paris: Librairie Felix Alcan.

Ethington, Philip J. 1997. The Intellectual Construction of 'Social Distance:' Toward a Recovery of Georg Simmel's Social Geometry. *Cybergeo: European Journal of Geography*. As Retrieved on November 25, 2018 from https://journals.openedition.org/cybergeo/227.

Lawrence, Bruce B. 2005. Intoduction to the 2015 Edition. In *The Muqaddimah*. Columbia: Columbia University Press.

Miller, Jacques-Alain. 2008. Extimacy. *The Symptom*. As Retrieved on November 25, 2018 from http://www.lacan.com/symptom/extimity.html.

Simmel, Georg. 1908. Quantitative Aspects of the Group. In *The Sociology of Georg Simmel*, trans. and ed. Kurt H. Wolff. New York: The Free Press.

Simmel, Georg. 1971. *Georg Simmel: On Individuality and Social Forms*, trans. and ed. Donald N. Levine. Chicago: University of Chicago Press.

Žižek, Slavoj. n.d. Antinomies of Pure Sexuation. As Retrieved on November 9, 2018 from http://theoryleaks.org/text/articles/slavoj-Žižek/antinomies-of-pure-sexuation/.

CHAPTER 6

Ways Forward

Abstract Rousselle offers two possible ways forward for American sociology. First, he posits a contemporary theoretical system from Alain Badiou. Badiou's theory of the "event," as the moment of a contingent encounter with the Real, disrupts the consistency of the imaginary social link. Thus, Badiou offers a sociology capable of working through the category of the Real. Second, Talcott Parsons, whose work was critiqued so forcefully by C. Wright Mills, offers us a possible way forward with psychoanalysis and "grand theory." It is only by developing insights such as these into Parsons' and Badiou's work that we stand to make any headway in sociological theory today. If we are not prepared to take the Real seriously then we shall continue to suffer from the same problems sociologists were charged with addressing in the first place.

Keywords The real · Lacanian psychoanalysis · Alain Badiou · Event · Talcott Parsons · Systems theory · Grand theory

Alain Badiou's Choice

Early American sociologists suffered from an inability to articulate the structuring influence of the real. Their rallying cry was W. I. Thomas' theorem: "if men define their situations as real, [then] they are real in their consequences" (1923: 571–572). The Thomas theorem

D. Rousselle, *Jacques Lacan and American Sociology*,
The Palgrave Lacan Series,
https://doi.org/10.1007/978-3-030-19726-1_6

was subsequently picked up and developed within America by Peter L. Berger and Thomas Luckmann in their classic book *The Social Construction of Reality* (1966). Berger developed "interpretive sociology" into the sociology of "constructionism," or "social constructionism." His claim was that not all constructions are equal. Some constructions in fact have more influence over social groups than others. Berger and Luckmann exposed the Thomas theorem as being operative primarily at the level of meaning. And then, at that level of meaning or discourse, there are battles over the construction of social reality. Berger and Luckmann's contributions helped to push sociology towards the study of language, but they were not able to resolve the problem of the imaginary framework of these constructions.

Erving Goffman, who was one of the most popular contemporary sociologists, took issue with the theorem in the first few pages of his later work *Frame Analysis* (1974). His position was not that the theorem was inaccurate but rather that it came to be interpreted in all sorts of ways by sociologists. The irony of this situation should be remarked upon: the theorem was meant to express the importance of interpretation in the social life of individuals, and yet, at the same time, it was the many diverse interpretations of the theorem by so many sociologists that caused problems. In any case, the theorem was initially meant to expose the individual's sense of reality as dependent upon his or her singular experience. What matters is the way people interpret the truth, because this interpretation has a real effect. The challenge of the theorem was meant to shift the emphasis from an account of truth that is objective, universal, and incontestable towards one where truth is related to the subject's imaginary knowledge.

A brief detour seems to me to be essential: the context within which the Thomas theorem was first presented has often been neglected by sociologists. Indeed, most sociologists are entirely unfamiliar with the context: the theorem—"if men define their situations as real, they are real in their consequences"—was presented only after an extended discussion of a case of paranoid psychosis. In other words, it was from the case of a man with "delusions" (in this case, delusions of persecutions) that the theorem emerged. I shall quote at length the key passage:

> A document prepared by one compensating for a feeling of inferiority or elaborating a delusion of persecution is as far as possible from objective reality, but the subject's view of the situation, how he regards it, may be

> the most important element for interpretation. For his immediate behavior is closely related to his definition of the situation, which may be in terms of objective reality or in terms of a subjective appreciation — 'as if' it were so. [...] To take an extreme example, the warden of Dannemora prison recently refused to honor the order of the court to send an inmate outside the prison walls for some specific purpose. He excused himself on the ground that the man was too dangerous. He had killed several persons who had the unfortunate habit of talking to themselves on the street. From the movement of their lips he imagined that they were calling him vile names, and he behaved as if this were true. If men define their situations as real, they are real in their consequences. (Thomas 1923: 572)

One should ask oneself why it is that the Thomas theorem used the case of a delusion to generate an axiom the likes of which became universally applicable to all those who do not suffer from delusions. There is implied in this extrapolation the claim that delusion is somewhere at the heart of the social bond; language, then, is the delusion of the subject against the intrusion of the real. Yet, this is not at all how delusion functions according to the Lacanian orientation. The category of "delusion" is reserved for very particular situations wherein the subject affirms, strongly, a sense of unwavering certainty over social reality (rather than, for example, a feeling of doubt). More recently, Jacques-Alain Miller has explored delusion as constitutive of subjectivity during the modern age. Miller (1995) wrote that "in the measure of what constitutes 'I' in each of us, there is the possibility that each of us is delusion." It is a subtle point but one well worth noting: delusions exist within neurotic structures as well as psychotic structure, and it should not be presumed that the mere presence of a delusion is the sole criteria by which to distinguish the various clinical structures. In other words, it is not that psychosis may be distinguished from neurosis by the mere presence of delusions. The subject, which is the unique privilege of neurotic structure, is itself a delusion made possible by the symbolic's intrusion into the real. It occurs when subjectivity is foreclosed or barred by the symbolic. The only remaining option for a subject which has been barred from the symbolic is to return within the real as a certainty (see Rousselle 2018).

The "real," as impossibility, as rupture, is also a reflecting surface upon which the subject's images—his or her ego, his or her knowledge—may be projected. This, after all, was Erving Goffman's lesson. It is no different from the real described by Jacques-Alain Miller in his preface to Lacan's *Television*: "one never understands anything but one's fantasies and one is never taught by anything other than what one doesn't understand, i.e., by nonsense" (Miller 1990: xxvi). The subject, when faced with the real of nonsense, or, to put it in another way, the real of the social relation, flees into the world of his imaginary fantasies, into his knowledge, his interpretations, his ego, his role, and so on; so afraid is he of organizing a new world around the principle of the rupture, he instead opts without fail for the comfort of the imaginary.

Slavoj Žižek contends that the real and the experience of "subjective destitution" are related: "what Lacan called 'subjective destitution' [is] an abrupt awareness of the utter meaninglessness of our social links, the dissolution of our attachment to [imaginary/symbolic] reality itself—all of a sudden, other people are derealized, reality itself is experienced as a confused whirlpool of shapes and sounds, so that we are no longer able to formulate our desire" (Žižek 2007). American sociologists have not engaged with the real of subjective destitution but have become too satisfied, indeed too fascinated, by roles, picture frames, looking glasses, situations, and gestures—and, consequently, at the meta-theoretical level they have not been able to advance beyond key debates in structure and agency, micrological and macrological sociology, and so on (see Ritzer 2008). For this reason, American sociologists will need to begin to engage with the work of the French philosopher Alain Badiou.

American sociologists have argued, forcefully, that there are imaginary foundations for symbolic agencies. The symbolic becomes rendered here as *semblance*. But they have not developed a compelling theory of the real (outside of "reality"). Alain Badiou has given the name "Event" for that moment when, within the imaginary social relationship, there is a contingent encounter, or, as Lacan has famously put it, a "touch of the real." Our provisional definition of an Event is the following: it is a moment when the impossible real interrupts or disrupts the consistency of the imaginary social link (indeed, of discourse itself). The Event thereby "subjectivizes" the subject, or, put another way, the Event makes possible subjectivity as such; since, as Badiou has claimed, there is no subject before an Event (see Badiou 2012: 103).

During this moment, when the subject is touched by an event, a choice opens up. The choice is only between a return to the imaginary consistency of the social situation, a return to prevailing social roles and identifications, or else a movement through the anxiety of an altogether different and unknown possibility. For Badiou, "an event is always the opening of a new possibility," it is always a "localized rupture in the [social] world" (2012: 29–30). An event is therefore always a disruption of the social bond rather than the forging of a social bond. It is the moment of truth, since, the difference between a Lacanian sociology and American sociology may very well be expressed in the following way: American sociology is addicted to quick imaginary fixes for the rupture in the social bond, while Lacanian sociology is interested in exploring the following axiom: *there is no such thing as a social relationship*. This is a modified version of the popular Lacanian axiom: "there is no such thing as a sexual relationship."

The moment when the subject is faced with a choice is also the moment when the subject as such arrives on the scene. This subjective choice is what Alain Badiou has named a "point." It is the responsibility of a subject to show "fidelity" to the event, by drawing out its implications, point by point. Andrew Robinson has put this most clearly when he wrote that "subjects show fidelity to an event [which] means that they interpret and explore an event without denying its evental nature" (Robinson 2015). The decision or choice is to face the rupture of the imaginary social bond from within the unique perspective of subjective destitution. It occurs during the moment when a subject becomes provoked by anxiety and finds himself split between the consistency of the situation (the imaginary) and the pure choice of a new situation (the real).

Badiou insists on the necessity of the classical logic of negation, which, in other words, is the logic of "revolution." When you face a decision you are within the revolutionary imperative of classical logic. Classical logic delivers the subject from the temptation: the temptation is always to destroy the new situation by saying "no" instead of "yes." A "point" is made during the war-time situation when the subject affirms that the question is one of either doing *this* or else doing *that*. If you do *that*, instead of *this*, then the whole revolutionary context becomes destroyed. More often, we are tempted to pursue the path of the easy decision instead of struggling with the "yes" of the revolutionary impulse. Very often within the neo-liberal capitalist context, the temptation is to do both *this* as well as *that* (to have your cake and eat it too) rather than to make a choice. It is at the level of compromise that the revolutionary context of classical logic becomes destroyed: to do *p* but to also do *not-p*.

First, there is the prevailing situation, which is marked by its imaginary consistency. However, beneath the consistency of appearances there are multiplicities imbued with possibility. The arrangement of these abstract multiplicities into any sort of consistency defines the situation as such. Second, there is an Event which ruptures that consistency. It is the surging forth of multiplicities from within the eventual occurrence. Third, the subject emerges as a consequence of his or her agency in response to the determination of this real Event. If the subject responds to the anxiety of that rupture with courage by facing it as a pure possibility then a new situation introduces itself. The subject is therefore charged with the task of articulating the truth or idea of the new situation. Truth is therefore not reducible to the prevailing situation or its various determinations. Rather, truth must appear there within and against the situation: "truth has a relationship to the negation [which is] an event […] it is creation […] Truth is the result of a [subjective] process of construction" (Badiou 2012: 114). The subject touched by the real of an event takes upon him or herself the difficult task of now rendering the situation—indeed, the entire world—according to the Event's lasting contribution.

The practical sociologist will wonder about the explanatory power of the preceding conceptual framework. He or she will ask a question concerning the practicality of the theory of the event. I shall provide a simple example of an Event, as I understand it. I am sometimes asked about my writing process. The situation of my writing is such that I begin writing about what I think I know. The consistency of my knowledge is often structured or authorized by a master figure such as Alain Badiou or Jacques Lacan. However, it soon becomes obvious, with luck, that there is a limit to the knowledge being presented. I stumble upon an unforeseen profound insight which comes to me as if out of nowhere, from within that limit; it appears to me first as nonsensical and unrelated. The challenge is therefore to explore its consequences as far as possible, though I know that it is an obstacle to the consistency of the work.

I remain in fidelity to the insight which goes beyond my knowledge, and which goes beyond my ability to comprehend its significance for my discourse. I exhaust its possibilities within the essay by rewriting and reorganizing the entire essay around the new possibility. And then I stitch up the essay piece by piece, point by point, until nothing in the manuscript has become untouched by the initial insight. Finally, you have before you the book. It was a book that began with an entirely different topic and an entirely different theme. It is now the book you hold in your hands.

Parsing Talcott Parsons

It certainly appears as though many key psychoanalytic contributions were already present within the work of the symbolic interactionists: the centrality of language for the formation of social bonds, the imaginary constitution of the self, the role of gestures, the generalized other, and significant symbols (signifiers), etc. The symbolic interactionists accepted some elements of Freudian thought, though often without realizing it, while rejecting others. Phillip Manning, an American sociologist, recently argued that "[it was believed that] elements of psychoanalysis [...] were [already] anticipated in some form by the founding figures of symbolic interactionism; [...] there were non-clinical but empirical ways of pursuing symbolic interactionism 'after Freud'" (Manning 2005: 2). If it is true that symbolic interactionism was the dominant paradigm at the time of the birth of American sociology, and if, moreover, it continues to be a leading paradigm, then for a short time we were faced with the possibility of another sociological paradigm: the "systems theory" or "structural functionalism" of Talcott Parsons.

However, the two "schools" of thought commonly associated with the work of Talcott Parsons have done more to hinder our understanding. What often happens within sociological theory courses in the United States and Canada is that the various schools of thought—"conflict theory," "post-structuralism," "postmodernism," "systems theory," "structural functionalism," and so on—go to war against one another. The sociologist typically abstracts from the work of the various thinkers and speaks at a level so general that it is no longer applicable to the sources from which the concepts sprang. Ironically, in this case, this was precisely the practice that C. Wright Mills sought to refute when he came up against the "grand theory" of Talcott Parsons. I contend that we go back to the drawing board, so to speak, by refusing to engage in hopeless and ineffectual dialogues about the various merits or drawbacks of the supposed "schools of sociology."

George Ritzer has claimed in his popular *Sociological Theory* textbook that American sociology was once synonymous with Parsonsian "systems theory" (Ritzer 2008: 230). It seems fairer to claim, as Turner did in his influential book on Talcott Parsons, that: "[Parsons'] influence in American professional sociology was both limited and short term" (Turner in Parsons 1991). Turner qualified his statement: "Parsons was somewhat remote from mainstream American sociology, which continued to be dominated by American academics such as Robert Park, Charles Cooley, Franklin Giddings, Albion Small, William Sumner, William Thomas, and Lester Ward" (Turner in Parsons 1991). But Parsons offered American sociologists another path, one that was neither the pragmatic "conflict" sociology of C. Wright Mills nor the pragmatic micrological sociology of the "symbolic interactionists": the path of systems theory, of structural functionalism, of being more interdisciplinary, and of grand theory.

Indeed, "grand theory" was not in itself the problem, despite Mills' insistence. Mills certainly made the phrase "grand theory" synonymous with "bad sociology," and he helped to contribute to a scholarly milieu that was opposed to abstraction and to sustained theoretical work (for being "disengaged" from "practical" concerns). Mills, in his *The Sociological Imagination* (1959), attacked Parsons directly as exemplary of a particular trend within American sociology. In the second chapter, Mills wrote: "Let us begin with a sample of grand theory, taken from Talcott Parsons' *The Social System*—widely regarded as a most important book by a most eminent representative of the style" (1959: 25). He continued: "[t]he fact is that [Grand Theory] is not readily understandable; the suspicion is that it may not be altogether intelligible" (1959: 26). It is possible that "grand theory" was a diagnosis that Mills made precisely on the basis of Parsons' work alone.

What Mills could not admit was that the price one pays for precision is a certain degree of conceptual abstraction: as Hegel famously put it, "it is the Concept itself which exists empirically" (Hegel as quoted in Kojeve 1980: 101). One might even wonder to what extent interdisciplinary is possible without risking some abstraction. Yet, it is curious that Mills resorted to the very concept of "grand theory" to better navigate the admittedly difficult and dense writings of Parsons. Is it not the case, then, that Mills favoured the development of a conceptual apparatus rather than a practical engagement with the environment, even though he, at the same time, wrote the following: "[c]laiming to set forth 'a general sociological theory,' the grand theorist in fact sets forth a realm of concepts from which are excluded many structural features of human society [...]" (Mills 1959: 35). This, precisely, was what Mills was forced to do in order to gain some knowledge about the text. A conceptual approach helps to provide some headway in the noise of the immediate environment, whether that environment is textual or, what perhaps amounts to the same thing, social.

What interests me is that Parsons was among very few American sociologists to have explored Freudian theory and technique both extensively and explicitly within his theory (Lupton 1997; Manning 2005). Parsons trained at the Boston Psychoanalytic Institute under Grete Bibring in 1946 and he frequently attended clinical psychoanalytic gatherings. Yet, at the same time, Parsons did not abandon the insights of symbolic interactionism. This is made most obvious in his discussion of the necessity of analysing the various functional components of the so-called "action system." Some sociologists have even claimed that Parsons' work advanced upon and developed key insights from the symbolic interactionist tradition (see, for example, Turner 1974). However, what many of the symbolic interactionists could not get behind was Parsons' argument that there is an independent structure—like Emile Durkheim's social structure, examined through "social facts"—which would determine, externally, and influence social behaviour, coercively, against the conscious will of the individual and his or her experience. As Turner put it:

> [S]ymbolic interactionists, following the work of Erving Goffman, also argued against what they took to be Parsons' functionalist account of social order. For symbolic interactionists, order was an emergent property of micro-social interaction, which could only be sustained by cooperative negotiation between social actors. The point was that social stability was inherently precarious. (Turner in Parsons 1974)

It is not my intention to defend Parsons from his American critics but rather to investigate Parsons encounter with the Freudian discovery. The problem as I see it was that Parsons reduced the contributions of psychoanalysis to only one or two of the various subsystems: the "personality" subsystem, and, to a lesser extent, the "behavioural" subsystem. Thus, psychoanalytic theory—like symbolic interactionist theory—was reduced in its explanatory role to a mere component of a larger interdisciplinary framework for any social or cultural system. As Davenport put it, "[m]ore than anything else [...] Parsons relied upon [...] psychoanalytic theory for the personality level of his theory of action" (1966: 275).

According to Parsons, the social system has four components, each taking on a unique functional imperative for the maintenance of the overall system. The behavioural system was responsible for adaptation of the individual to its real environment. In this respect, we might think about the economy: individuals adapt to their environment by collecting and working with the raw resources of a given milieu. The personality system sets goals for the individual; we may imagine the political apparatus as being responsible, in this sense, for setting goals on economic labour. The social system—composed almost entirely of those same agencies listed by Althusser in his "ideological state apparatus" essay—brings together conflicting interests. Finally, the cultural system, which exists at the highest level of society, consists of attempts to keep cultural meanings in play by transmitting them to new elements within the overall system (Table 6.1).

The psychoanalytic theory of transference was related essentially to issues of "object choice" for Parsons, which, for him, was already a decision made within the corpus of psychoanalytic interpretations of Freud. For example, within "Social Structure and the Development of Personality" [1958], Parsons claimed that Freud's major contribution to sociology could be:

> [H]is organization of the personality as a system; and the relation of the individual to his social milieu, especially in the process of personality development. Thus, in psychoanalytic terminology, is the field of 'object relations' — the most important area of articulation between the analytic theory of the personality of the individual and the sociological theory of the structure and functioning of social system. (Parsons [1958] 2016: 321)

I would like to highlight some major concepts in the preceding passage: "organization," "system," "individual," and "object." All of these concepts demonstrate a commitment to the understanding of *imaginary* qualities of the individual, that is, the individual's consistency, the organization of the individual as an ego-object, who relates to others as objects within their imaginary dimension. In a previous chapter,

Table 6.1 Talcott Parsons' systems

Component: Behavioural subsystem Function: Adaptation Component: Cultural subsystem Function: Pattern maintenance	Component: Personality subsystem Function: Goal attainment Component: Social subsystem Function: Integration

I referred to this as the *a*-to-*a'* relation: it is the plane of transference, of the imaginary. This was Parsons' missed opportunity: he was motivated to demonstrate the social applicability of Freud's discovery, and, to do so he was required to devalue the "real" Freud. And this, precisely, was what Parsons did when he opened his paper:

> The primary emphasis in interpreting Freud's work — at least in the United States — has tended to be on the power of the individual's instinctual needs and the deleterious effects of their frustration. [...] The consequence of such a trend is to interpret Freud as a psychologist who brought psychology closer to the biological sciences, and to suggest the relative unimportance of society and culture, except as these constitute agencies of the undesirable frustration of man's instinctual needs. (Ibid.)

Parsons could not conceive of a non-biological version of the "real" which is nonetheless embodied, that is, he could not foresee within Freud's work—indeed, made most apparent in his *Beyond the Pleasure Principle* (1920)—a "real" that would contribute not only to the subject's frustration but also and more essentially to the formation of the social system. Indeed, sociologists continue to focus on the supposedly "biological" version of the instincts in Freud's work (see the popular textbook, *The Social Construction of Sexuality* by Steven Seidman 2014). Yet, by implication, this possibility offered itself to Parsons since his action systems were arranged in a certain logical order which highlighted the centrality of biological resources (adaptation, which, in this case, could have also meant adaptation with the "real") for the formation of higher levels of culture. Put differently, the real "event" could have been seen as a useless "resource" in the adaptation subsystem.

Parsons arranged the various systems in terms of their various levels of influence. He maintained that the behavioural subsystem provides the "resources" for the higher level systems, and the cultural subsystem provides the "power" over the lower level systems. We might arrange the systems in the following way (Table 6.2).

The event may interfere with the resources of power and push themselves towards the transcendental level of culture through the personality and social systems.

In any case, the "object relations" interpretation of Freud's work came under intense criticism by Jacques Lacan during his early seminars. His problem was that the school of object relations—which, within the

Table 6.2 Talcott Parsons' system levels

Resources (high)		Power (low)
	Behavioural	
	Personality	
	Social	
	Cultural	
Resources (low)		Power (high)

United States was always situated in a false conflict with "ego psychology" (Mitchell 1997: 101)—moved away from Freud's most important discovery: the unconscious. Lacan summarized his critique with unusual clarity: "the imaginary link established in the transference bears a very close relation to the notion of the object relation" (Lacan [1953] 1991: 111). He continued, "[t]he object relation must always submit to the narcissistic framework and be inscribed in it" (Lacan [1953] 1991: 111). It is at this point that Lacan makes the case that the object relation is always an imaginary relation, and, moreover, it always produces for the subject a situation of love. We need to be very careful here because for Lacan love is a double-edged sword and the object relation exposes one of the problems of love: it is what makes up for the lack of a (social) relation. In his fourth seminar, he said:

> [W]e cannot pose the problem of the object relation correctly unless we begin with a certain framework that must be considered as fundamental […]. This framework, or the first of these frameworks, is that in the human world, the lack of the object provides the structure as well as the beginning of objectal organization. This lack of the object must be conceived at its different stages in the subject — with regard to the symbolic chain, which escapes him in its beginning as in its end — at the level of frustration [the imaginary], where he is in fact installed in a lived experience that is unthinkable for him — but we must also consider this lack in the real […]. (Lacan 2018: 53)

Lacan's point was that Freud wasn't chiefly concerned with the object but rather with the *lack of an object*, that is, with castration anxiety or the lack of the phallus (sometimes described as "minus-phi"). It was this conviction that led Lacan to his own discovery, one which, at times Lacan goes to great length to argue was his major contribution to the Freudian field: the *objet petit a*. No wonder Jacques-Alain Miller, in the preface to Lacan's *Television*, wrote:

> The fact, if you can believe it, is that "Ego Psychology" — stemming from the work of Anna Freud and Heinz Hartmann — still predominates in America; as a Chicago analyst was telling me yesterday, it has become like wallpaper for American analysts: it's so much in evidence that no one pays attention to it anymore. Ego psychology so thoroughly deflected Freud's work from its authentic perspective that it is currently suffering the return of what it rejected in the guise of "object relations theory," which is no less partial. (Miller 1990: xxx)

Instead of focusing on the real frustrations of individuals—that is, of the frustrations of ego and image—the object relations theorists seemed to be interested in the proper organization of imaginary consistencies. The paradox is that Parsons attempted to move away from a focus on real frustration only to find that overcome the real frustrations of consistencies, of systems and organizations, was at the heart of his project. The consequence was that "the object [for the object relations theorists becomes] first and foremost is an object of satisfaction" (Lacan 1988: 209). Rodriquez summarized all of this:

> What Lacan has emphasized is the radical, absolute character of the loss of the object, in that this object (at the level of drive as well as desire) is constituted as forever lost: it is not that the subject once had it and then lost it, but rather that the subject can only 'have' it as lost, as pure lack [...] Thus, for Lacan, the object relation is the relation with the lack of the object. (Rodriquez 1999: 122)

In "Psychoanalysis and the Social Structure," Parsons argued that "if the sociologist is to utilize the potential contributions of psychoanalysis to his problems, he can only do so competently by going to the authentic sources, by learning psychoanalysis himself, as far as possible by the regular training procedures" (1971: 346). This was what Parsons did. However, he presumed that psychoanalysis was reducible to a field of knowledge, which, in other words, is an imaginary understanding of psychoanalysis—as if it is to focus on Freud's *ego*—and neglects the real of psychoanalytic technique. Parsons' solution to dealing with the gap that separates psychoanalysis from sociology was to "put it into a frame of reference," that is, to relegate it to one of the subsystems of inquiry, namely the "personality" subsystem.

Parsons took as his point of departure, before moving any further, a discrepancy or disjuncture, between the "personality system" and the "social system," attributing psychoanalytic knowledge to any understanding of the former and sociological knowledge to the latter. It is this disjuncture that I find most curious because it demonstrates, or renews rather, and without Parsons fully realizing it, the real of the social relation as impossible. If it is true, as many sociologists have pointed out over the years, that Society is just another name for "superego," or for the Lacanian Other, then why is it that there is no relationship among the personality and the Other? This is curious, to say the least. Parsons wrote at the beginning of his essay on "Psychoanalysis and the Social System":

> There are two main foci of theoretical organization of systems within the broad framework of this conceptual scheme. One is the individual personality as a system, and the other is the social system. [...] It is extremely important to differentiate the various levels and ways in which these conceptual components are involved or combined. It is dangerous to shift from the one level to the other without taking adequate account of the systematic differences that are involved. (1971: 336–337)

He ends his essay with a similar point. There is a "gap" separating psychoanalytic inquiry into human motivations or personality and the subject matter of sociology—and yet sociology and psychoanalysis, being two different points of view must nonetheless listen to one another without overcoming the gap: "can [the psychoanalyst] in the long run do without [the contributions of sociology] any more than the sociologist can do without the insights of psychoanalysis?" (Parsons 1971: 347).

It is only by developing these insights into Parsons and Badiou's work that we stand to make any headway in sociology today. Unfortunately, without taking the *real* serious, as an agency independent of the imaginary, we shall continue to suffer from the same problem we are charged with addressing.

References

Badiou, Alain. 2012. *The Subject of Change*, ed. Duane Rousselle. New York, NY: Atropos Press.

Berger, Peter L., and Thomas Luckmann. 1966. *The Social Construction of Reality.* New York: Penguin Random House Books.

Freud, Sigmund. 1920. *Beyond the Pleasure Principle 1922*, trans. C. J. M. Hubback and ed. Pref. Ernest Jones, viii + 90. London and Vienna: International Psycho-Analytical Press.

Goffman, Erving. 1974. *Frame Analysis: An Essay on the Organization of Experience*. Boston: Northeastern University Press.

Kojeve, Alexandre. 1980. *Introduction to the Reading of Hegel: Lectures on the Phenomenology of Spirit*, trans. James H. Nichols, Jr. and ed. Allan Bloom. Ithaca: Cornell University Press.

Lacan, Jacques. 1988. *The Seminar of Jacques Lacan, Book I: Freud's Papers on Technique*, trans. John Forrester and ed. Jacuqes-Alain Miller. New York and Cambridge: Cambridge University Press.

Lacan, Jacques. [1953] 1991. *The Seminar of Jacques Lacan, Book I: Freud's Papers on Technique*, trans. John Forrester and ed. Jacques-Alain Miller. New York: W. W. Norton.

Lacan, Jacques. 2018. *The Seminar of Jacques Lacan, Book IV: The Object Relation* (unknown translation, private copy).

Lupton, Deborah. 1997. Psychoanalytic Sociology and the Medical Encounter: Parsons and Beyond. *Sociology of Health & Illness* 19 (5): 561–579.

Manning, Philip. 2005. *Freud & American Sociology*. New York: Polity.

Miller, Jacques-Alain. 1990. Micro-scopia: An Introduction to the Reading of Television. In *Television: A Challenge to the Psychoanalytic Establishment*, trans. Denis Hollier, Rosalind Krauss, Annette Michelson, and Jeffrey Mehlmen and ed. Joan Copjec, xi–xxx. New York, NY: W. W. Norton.

Miller, Jacques-Alain. 1995. The Invention of Delusion. In *International Lacanian Review*, trans. G.-S. Marshall. As Retrieved on April 12, 2017 from http://www.lacancircle.net/JAMinventionofdelusion.pdf.

Mills, C. Wright. 1959. *The Sociological Imagination*. Oxford: Oxford University Press.

Mitchell, Stephen A. 1997. *Influence and Autonomy in Psychoanalysis*. New York, NY: Routledge.

Parsons, Talcott. 1971. *The System of Modern Societies*. Engelwood Cliffs, NJ: Prentice-Hall.

Parsons, Talcott. 1991. *The Social System*, ed. Bryan S. Turner. London: Routledge.

Parsons, Talcott. [1958] 2016. Social Structure and the Development of Personality: Freud's Contribution to the Integration of Psychology and Sociology. *Psychiatry: Interpersonal and Biological Processes* 21 (4): 321–340.

Ritzer, George. 2008. *Sociological Theory* (8th ed.). New York: McGraw Hill.

Robinson, Andrew. 2015. Alain Badiou: Truth, Subjectivity, and Fidelity. *Ceasefire*. January 20, 2015. As Retrieved on July 17, 2018 from https://ceasefiremagazine.co.uk/alain-badiou-truth-subjectivity-fidelity/.

Rodriquez, L. S. 1999. Lacan's Subversion of the Subject. In *Psychoanalysis with Children*, ed. L. S. Rodriquez. London: Free Association.

Rousselle, Duane. 2018. A Portrait of Baudelaire as a 'Man of Genius': Ordinary Psychosis Within the Age of Modernity. *Psychoanalysis Lacan* 3. See http://psychoanalysislacan.com/.

Seidman, Steven. 2014. *The Social Construction of Sexuality*. New York, NY: W. W. Norton.

Thomas, William Isaac, and Dorothy Thomas. 1923. *The Child in America: Behavior Problems and Programs*. New York: Knopf.

Turner, Johnathan H. 1974. Parsons as a Symbolic Interactionist: A Comparison of Action and Interaction Theory. *Sociological Inquiry* 44 (4): 283–294.

Žižek, Slavoj. 2007. Only a Suffering God Can Save Us. *Lacanian Ink*. As Retrieved on July 29, 2018 from http://www.lacan.com/zizshadowplay.html.

Index

A
The Act, 55, 56
Action system (Parsons), 85, 87
Actor network theory, 5
Adab, 72
Addiction(s), 34, 35, 37
Althusser, Louis, 36, 86
American Sociological Association (ASA), 12, 42
Analytic discourse, 2, 3
Anti-Positivism, 67
Arranged marriage, 50
'asabiyyah, 13, 70, 71
At-least-one, 68
At-least-one (Lacan), 71

B
Badaah, 73
Badiou, Alain, 7, 13, 26, 69, 73, 74, 77, 80–82
Baudelaire, Charles, 51
Berger, Peter L., 78
Beyond the Pleasure Principle (Sigmund Freud), 7, 44, 87
Biology, 7, 51
Blackmar, Frank Wilson, 12
Black Mirror, 35
Blumer, Herbert, 42
Boston Psychoanalytic Institute, 85
Bryant, Levi, 32
Burn-out, 33
Bush, George W., 27, 69
Butler, Judith, 55

C
Capitalism, 4, 5, 18, 25, 27, 30, 31, 33, 34, 49, 67
Capitalist discourse, 5, 18, 19, 24, 27, 29, 31–34, 49, 50, 64
Carrey, Jim, 58
Cash-value, 4, 5, 54
Castration, 3, 4, 17–20, 26, 28, 54, 55, 63, 71, 72, 74, 88
Censor, 43, 44

D. Rousselle, *Jacques Lacan and American Sociology*, The Palgrave Lacan Series,
https://doi.org/10.1007/978-3-030-19726-1

Clark University, 14
Coca-Cola, 27
Cognitive behavioural therapy, 15
Comte, Auguste, 11, 12, 62, 65
Conflict theory, 2, 13, 83
Consistency, 2, 3, 5, 6, 20, 24, 47, 48, 80–82, 86
Conspiracy theories, 20
Cynicism, 57

D
Dean, Jodi, 37
Death-drive, 50
Decisional structure, 3, 6
Delusion, 78, 79
Demand, 2–5, 43, 49, 63
de Saussure, Ferdinand, 16, 45, 46, 73
Desire, 15, 24, 30, 34, 37, 51, 68, 72, 80, 89
Dewey, John, 20, 41
Dialectical behavioural therapy, 15
Disavowal, 4, 17, 19, 20, 26, 37
Discourse, 1–7, 14–17, 19, 20, 25, 27, 30–33, 41, 45, 48, 49, 57, 65, 68, 71, 73, 74, 78, 80, 82
Distance, 6, 34, 56, 65, 68, 70, 71
Durkheim, Emile, 13, 62, 65, 66, 85
Dyad/Triad, 68

E
Ego, 3, 15, 29, 43, 47, 48, 53, 57, 69, 79, 80, 88, 89
Ego-ideal/Ideal-ego, 42, 43
Empty set (Set theory), 68
Enjoyment (Jouissance), 34, 37
Event, 73, 74, 80–82, 87
Event (Alain Badiou), 73, 74, 80–82
Event (ibn Khaldun), 71, 73, 74
Extimacy, 69

F
Facebook, 26, 37
Father, 14, 17, 27, 33, 44, 48, 50, 51, 54, 65, 66, 68, 71
Fidelity (Alain Badiou), 81
Foreclosure, 16, 17, 19, 31
Frames, 80
Freemasonry, 20
Freud, Anna, 89
Freud, Sigmund, 7, 11, 14, 15, 18, 41, 43–47, 50, 51, 54, 62, 63, 68, 71, 74, 83, 86–89
Frustration, 87–89
Fukuyama, Francis, 27

G
Gadgets, 5, 33
Gadgets (apps), 5, 33
Game stage/Play stage, 47
Gaze, 20, 55, 74
Generalized other, 46–48, 83
Gesture(s), 7, 8, 45, 46, 51, 52, 63, 80, 83
God, 37, 66
Grand theory, 8, 83, 84
Gravity, 56
Grey's Anatomy, 23, 24
Grigg, Russell, 26

H
Hall, G. Stanley, 14, 41
Hartmann, Heinz, 89
Having & Not having, 13
Hegel, 84
Hole, 16, 17, 27, 65
Hypersexuality, 34
Hysterical neurosis, 24

I

Ideal-type, 66, 67
Id/Ego/Superego, 3, 15, 29, 43, 47, 48, 53, 57, 69, 71, 79, 80, 88–90
Identity, 64
Ideology, 3, 6, 7, 25, 28, 29, 36, 37
Image, 3, 7, 8, 15, 20, 26, 29, 31, 32, 42, 45, 52, 54–56, 89
Imaginary, 3, 7, 8, 15, 20, 24–27, 30, 31, 35, 43–49, 51, 53–57, 64, 78, 80, 81, 83, 86, 88–90
Impossible, 80, 90
Instagram, 26
Instrumental rationality, 28
Intersectionality, 5
Introjection, 47

J

James, William, 4, 7, 21, 41
Jameson, Fredric, 25, 27
Journal of Sociology, 12

K

Kaur, Rupi, 28
Kitsch, 28
Klein bottle, 36
Knavery/Foolishness, 72
Knowledge, 1–3, 5, 6, 16, 19, 20, 37, 44, 49, 52–54, 62, 73, 74, 78–80, 82, 84, 89, 90

L

Lack, 2, 26, 37, 52, 55, 68, 72, 88, 89
Lalangue, 29
Language, 3, 13, 17, 45, 49, 51, 52, 66, 68, 70, 71, 78, 79, 83
Laruelle, Francois, 3
Lathouses, 30, 32
Light Phone, 32, 33
Little Hans, 54
Lombardi, Mark, 26, 27
Looking-glass self, 52, 53
Loose, Rik, 37
Love, 28, 49, 50, 88
Luckmann, Thomas, 78

M

Mark/Trace (Alain Badiou), 26, 73, 74
Marx, Karl, 13, 62
Mask, 7, 55, 57
Master discourse, 25
Maternal voice, 28, 29
McDonalds, 28, 29
Me, 42–44, 46, 48, 51
Mental market, 15
Miller, Jacques-Alain, 3, 15–19, 69, 79, 80, 88, 89
Mills, C. Wright, 2, 8, 12, 13, 83, 84
Mindfulness, 15
Mirror stage, 52, 55
Modernization, 28

N

Name-of-the-father, 16, 17, 19, 24, 25, 37, 44, 49, 51, 54, 66, 67, 71
Navel of the dream, 44, 45
Neurosis, 16, 18, 19, 79
Non-part, 2, 5, 13, 62
Non-philosophy, 3
Non-rapport, 31, 32
Not-all, 63

O

Object relations, 53, 86, 87, 89
Objet petit a, 34, 62, 65, 71, 88
Obsessional neurosis, 24
Ordinary psychosis, 17, 18

Other, 4, 12, 13, 15–18, 25–27, 30–34, 37, 43–48, 51–54, 58, 62, 65–69, 73, 74, 78–81, 89, 90

P
Park, Robert, 57, 84
Paternal function, 7, 49, 54
Performance, 49, 55, 56
Perversion, 17–19, 37
Phallocentrism, 71
Phallus, 4, 24, 71, 72, 88
Phantasy, 65
Phillip Manning, 83
Phobia/Phobic object, 54
Plato's cave, 36
Pleasure Principle, 7, 44, 87
Point (Alain Badiou), 81
Positivism, 65
Postmodernism, 25, 83
Post-structuralism, 83
Pragmatism, 3, 4, 6, 21, 41, 42
Projection, 47, 48
Proper name, 11, 14–16, 19, 27
Prosumer capitalism, 5
Psychiatry, 15
Psychosis, 16–19, 78, 79

Q
Qualitative research, 6
Quantitative research, 6
Queer theory, 5
Quran, 36, 37, 70

R
Ranciere, Jacques, 13, 62
The real, 3, 7, 8, 24, 26, 27, 37, 44, 45, 47, 50, 51, 53, 55, 56, 63, 72, 74, 77, 79–82, 87–90
Reality principle, 45
Religion, 70
Repression, 19
Ritzer, George, 12, 28, 42, 62, 80, 83
Robinson, Andrew, 81
Roles, 7, 23, 48, 55, 80
Rosenthal, Franz, 73

S
Said, Edward, 64
Secrecy, 68
Seidman, Steven, 87
Seinfeld, Jerry, 30
Semblance, 8, 17, 18, 20, 47, 48, 71, 72, 80
Semblant, 26, 32
Semiotics, 16, 71
Sex, 31, 34, 49, 50, 63
Sexuality, 23–25, 31, 33, 34
Sexuation, 63–65, 70, 71
Significant symbol, 7, 42, 45, 51, 52, 83
Signifier(s), 16, 17, 19, 20, 24, 26, 27, 30, 31, 37, 45–47, 49, 51, 52, 66, 73, 83
Social bond (Social link), 6, 7, 20, 27, 35, 49, 65, 66, 70
Social constructionism, 78
Social fact, 66, 67, 85
Social fact (Emile Durkheim), 66, 85
Social form, 65–68
Social geometry, 13, 62, 68
Social integration/Social regulation, 66
Social media, 25, 26, 32, 33, 35
Social self, 42, 48, 53
Society for the Study of Symbolic Interactionism (SSSI), 42
Spencer, Herbert, 2, 11, 12, 14
Split-subject, 31
Structural functionalism, 83, 84
Structuralism, 57, 83

Subjective division, 20, 33
Subjectivization (Alain Badiou), 81
Suicide, 66, 67
Sumner, William Graham, 11, 84
Super-ego, 32, 43, 68
Svolos, Thomas, 15, 30
Symbolic, 7, 17, 24–27, 29, 35, 43–45, 47, 48, 51, 53–55, 57, 63–67, 71, 74, 79, 80, 88
Symbolic efficacy, 54
Symbolic interactionism, 2, 4, 14, 41, 42, 49, 83, 85
Symptom, 8, 65
Systems theory, 2, 83, 84

T
Terrorism, 69, 70
Thomas, W.I., 77, 79
Thomas theorem, 77–79
Tomsic, Samo, 31
Topology, 13, 62, 68
Tradition, 4, 8, 12, 13, 18, 61–64, 67, 73, 74, 85
Transference, 86–88
Truth, 4, 7, 8, 20, 24, 25, 31, 72–74, 78, 81, 82
Truth (Alain Badiou), 7, 74, 81, 82

U
Unary trait, 51, 52
The uncanny, 62, 74
Unconscious, 4, 6, 8, 19, 34, 53, 65, 69, 74, 88
University discourse, 2, 3, 5, 62, 64, 67
Up-keying/Down-keying, 56

V
Vanheule, Stijn, 18, 20
Verstehen, 66
Voruz, Veronique, 51

W
Ward, Lester, 2, 12, 84
Warhol, Andy, 25
Wark, McKenzie, 36
Weber, Max, 28, 62, 66, 67
The woman does not exist, 64
Word art, 28
Wundt, Wilhelm, 41, 45

Z
Žižek, Slavoj, 6, 18–20, 25, 27, 29, 34, 63, 80
Zupancic, Alenka, 55

FSC
www.fsc.org
MIX
Papier | Fördert
gute Waldnutzung
FSC® C083411

Kolibri 360 GmbH
Ferdinand-Jühlke-Straße 7
99095 Erfurt, Deutschland
produktsicherheit@kolibri360.de